THE ROMAN EMPIRE

Published in 1996 by
Marshall Cavendish Corporation
99 White Plains Road
Tarrytown, NY 10591-9001
U.S.A.

Editor: Henk Dijkstra
Executive Editor: Paulien Retèl
Revision Editor: Henk Singor
Art Director: Henk Oostenrijk, Studio 87, Utrecht, The Netherlands
Index Editors: Schuurmans & Jonkers, Leiden, The Netherlands
Preface: Tracy L. Ehrlich, PhD, Dept. of Archaeology and Art History,
Columbia University, New York

The History of the Ancient and Medieval World is a completely revised and
updated edition of *The Adventure of Mankind*.
© 1996 HD Communication Consultants BV, Hilversum,
The Netherlands

Library of Congress Cataloging-in-Publication Data

History of the ancient and medieval world / edited by Henk Dijkstra.
p. cm.
Completely rev. and updated ed. of: The Adventure of mankind (second edition 1995).
Contents: —v.6. The Roman Empire.
ISBN 0-7614-0357-4 (v.6). — ISBN 0-7614-0315-5 (lib.bdg.:set)
1. History, Ancient—Juvenile literature. 2. Middle Ages—History—Juvenile literature. I. Dijkstra, Henk. II. Title: Adventure of mankind
D117.H57 1996
930—dc20/95-35715

History of the Ancient & Medieval World

Volume 6

The Roman Empire

Marshall Cavendish
New York Toronto Sydney

The Roman Empire

Roman houses with porticos on the bay of Naples. Fresco from Pompeii, AD 35-45

CONTENTS

Preface

The first century BC saw the end of the Roman Republic. First Pompey and then Julius Caesar gathered authority in the hands of one man. Power passed from the Senate and the Roman people to an absolute ruler. Noted for their military as well as political prowess, Pompey and Caesar brought the Mediterranean under Roman hegemony. By the end of the century, Rome controlled territories stretching from Asia Minor to the Iberian peninsula.

Augustus, the first Roman emperor, brought peace to the lands conquered by his predecessors. Under his rule literature and the arts flourished. The emperor embarked on an ambitious building program in Rome. Together with Roman political and administrative institutions, Augustan art and architecture were transported throughout the empire, solidifying the central authority of Rome. At the same time Augustus continued the military campaigns of his forebears, completing the subjugation of Spain and Germany as far as the Rhine.

Augustus was the first of the Julio-Claudian dynasty. His successors completed the solidification of the empire, centralizing the collection of taxes and all other administrative matters in the imperial authority located in the city of Rome. After the excesses of Caligula and Nero, who watched the city of Rome burn and built a sumptuous palace for himself upon its ashes, the Flavians based their rule upon concern for the Roman masses. On the site of Nero's palace, Vespasian initiated the construction of an amphitheater, later known as the Colosseum, to accommodate the gladitorial combats that fed the appetite of the bloodthirsty populace.

The second century AD dawned under the rule of Trajan, whose first priority lay in his military command. Through the conquest of Mesopotamia and Dacia, in northern Europe, he extended the already vast limits of the empire. His adopted son and successor, Hadrian, rejected aggression in favor of defense. The result was a fortified wall that bore his name, stretching across the Roman frontier in Britain (Britannia). His primary interest lay in cultural pursuits, and once again, as under Augustus, the arts flourished.

By late in the century, however, cracks had appeared in the Roman Empire. The Severan dynasty ruled as despots, their control threatened by civil wars throughout the empire, from North Africa to Asia Minor. The Persians, Goths, and Franks pressed Roman borders from all sides. The economy disintegrated and disease was rampant. Chaos reigned until the ascension of Diocletian, who reorganized the administration of the empire. While Diocletian ruled the east, he appointed a coemperor to rule the west. Each was supported by a second-in-command destined to succeed him. The sharing of power was short-lived, however, and Constantine the Great soon emerged as sole ruler. With his conversion to Christianity just prior to his death, he altered the course of history.

Tracy L. Ehrlich, PhD
Department of Art History and Archaeology
Columbia University, New York

Detail of a marble altar, showing soldiers in uniform and Romans dressed in togas

The End of the Republic

A Turbulent Time in Rome

The end of the Roman Republic was a turbulent time. Power was shifting from the Senate and Roman people to the hands of an absolute ruler. There were many twists and turns in this process and many historical figures played their part.

Lucius Sulla was an important one. He had been consul when he received the command of the military and was charged with subduing Mithridates VI, king of Pontus on the Black Sea. Mithridates had invaded the provinces of Asia and Greece in 88 BC, where he slaughtered Roman residents. Sulla waged a successful campaign against Mithridates in 86 BC and forged a peace treaty in 85 BC. Sulla was subsequently appointed dictator when he returned and invaded Italy, occupying Rome in 82 BC.

As 80 BC began, Sulla stepped down from the dictatorship, officially ending the state of emergency he had declared with his occupation two years earlier. His victory in 82 BC had ended the ongoing civil war. His reign of terror, legalized by his "proscriptions" (regulations he had written), had worked. Through them, he had legitimized the killing of hundreds of his opponents without trial and the seizing of their property to reward his supporters. His goal had been the restoration of the Senatus Populusque Romanus (the Senate and the Roman People) to its proper sovereignty. He had succeeded, restoring a stable oligarchy (government by the rich) under the Senate and its wealthy conservative party, the Optimates.

Membership in the Senate had depended on admission by the censors, two high-ranking senators normally elected at five-year intervals. In the past, they would review the list of *quaestors* (who handled public financial matters) and admit those of adequate moral stature to the Senate. Under Sulla, the achievement of quaestorship guaranteed admission into the Senate. The censors would also review the list of incumbent senators and expel any who had incurred *infamia*, or a bad public reputa-tion. They would then publish the new list of senators. Placement on it was critical to power; the first man named (and it was always a man) was *princeps Senatus* (first Senator), invited to speak first in all debate.

Sulla reduced the power of the censors and packed the Senate itself with 300 sup-porters. This, in turn, undermined the in-fluence in the Senate of the *equites* (equestrian order), the rank drawn from cavalry and business. He had already purged this class of any opposition to him, using his lethal proscriptions. Sulla, above all else, sought to reinstate traditional authority, both political and social. His technique was to eliminate all opposition. He wanted, and obtained, the support of the political nobility, or the *nobilitas* (the governing aristocracy) which was vitally interested in reestablishing its oligarchic republic. (The nobiles were the families whose members filled high offices of state.)

He likewise sought the support of the *gentes* who, tracing descent from a com-mon ancestor, comprised the backbone of Roman society. Centuries earlier, the most powerful gentes had begun to constitute a *patriciate* (a class based on lineage or fami-lial reputation). They established, as well, their *clientes*, or clients, who gave vo-ting allegiance in return for favors and personal assistance of all kinds.

The system of clientela, which reinforced the dependency relationship of the under-privileged on the privileged, was extended to foreigners. Both subjects and royalty in conquered regions were accorded Roman citizenship and the protection of dominant families in Rome in return for votes.

Below both gentes and their clients were the *plebeians* (of the plebs class), a polyglot group initially lacking all rights and responsibilities. (Military service and taxation were obligatory for the higher classes.) Since the fifth century, the plebeians had managed to circumvent patrician power through their own tribunate; in 494 BC, they established their assembly, the *concilium plebis*. It was established with a right of veto (only within the city limits of Rome itself) over the decision-making process of the consuls, the popular assemblies, and the Senate. Sulla, in his effort to enhance the Senate, diminished the authority of that tribunate of the plebs.

He also subjected the *praetors*, magi-strates charged with the administration of justice, to greater Senate control. The result was the dismantling of the jury reform of Gaius Gracchus, who had been tribune of

Political developments in the eastern part of the Mediterranean Sea from 90 BC to 60 BC

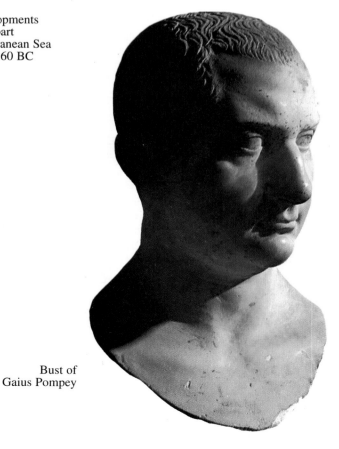

Bust of Gaius Pompey

the plebs in 123-122 BC. The Senate once again controlled the criminal courts.

Sulla retired, gambling that his massive attempt at the restoration of Senate prestige and authority would carry on. In fact, it was a failure. He died as a private citizen in 78 BC.

The most serious challenge to the system he established came from Quintus Sertorius. Refusing to join in the dictator's invasion of Italy in 82 BC, Sertorius had gone to southern Spain. Claiming to represent the legitimate Roman government, he set up a "counter-Senate" of prominent Roman citizens. An honest and fair administrator, he won native support over most of the Iberian peninsula. Despite his limited numbers and resources, he defeated three Roman armies in quick succession.

Pompey: Ascent to Power

In Rome, the Senate authorized a special command for the youthful Gnaeus Pompeius (Pompey), civil war ally of Sulla, to bring down Sertorius. To the embarrassment of the much larger Roman army, it took Pompey

The Temple of Hercules, built at the Forum Boarium, the oldest market place in Rome, in the first century BC. Greek influence is evident in the temple's rounded form and ornamentation.

This scene, made of Roman terracotta (a red-brown clay), depicts gladiators fighting lions in the circus, watched by spectators in the stands.

729

five years to do it. Only after Sertorius was assassinated by his own men in 72 BC were the remaining rebels destroyed.

The Roman army was stretched thin. Another major war had begun in Bithynia, Asia Minor. King Mithridates, ignoring the peace terms arranged by Sulla, challenged Rome. In 74 BC, the Senate acted again, sending the outstanding Optimate Consul Lucius Lucullus in as commander.

The Senate also gave Marcus Antonius (father of the later Roman ruler) naval command against the pirates destroying trade in the eastern Mediterranean.

Spartacus: Slave Rebellion

With the Roman army fighting on so many fronts, an unprecedented event in Italy took on major importance. In 73 BC, a revolt by the slaves of the gladiator school in Capua succeeded. Led by Spartacus, thousands of slaves escaped to form an army so powerful

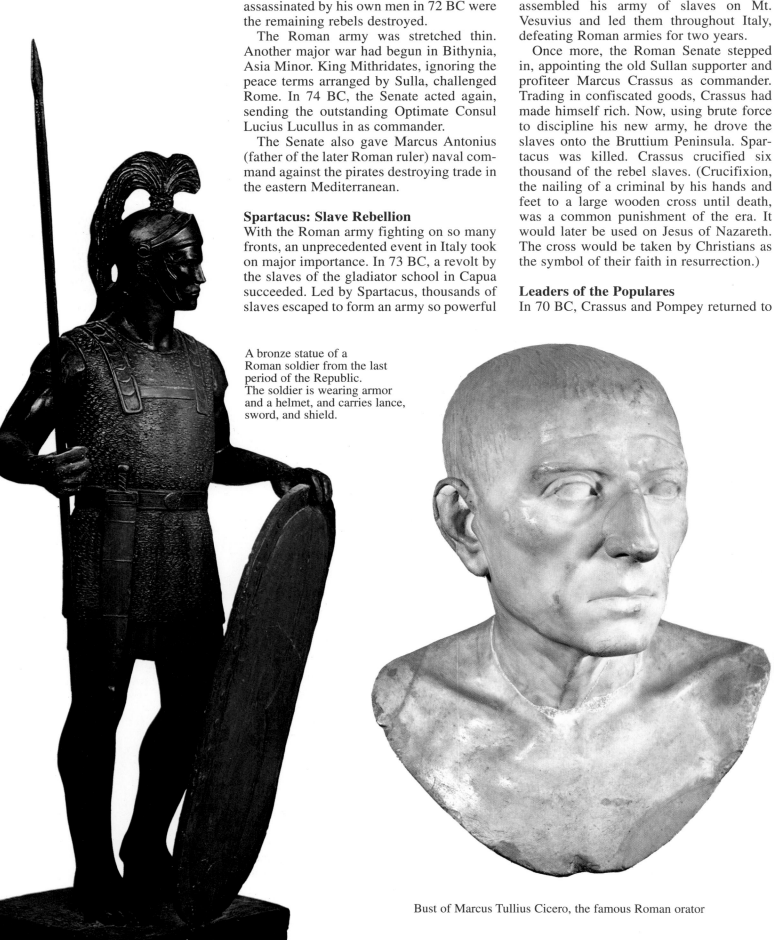

A bronze statue of a Roman soldier from the last period of the Republic. The soldier is wearing armor and a helmet, and carries lance, sword, and shield.

it brought down two consuls. Spartacus assembled his army of slaves on Mt. Vesuvius and led them throughout Italy, defeating Roman armies for two years.

Once more, the Roman Senate stepped in, appointing the old Sullan supporter and profiteer Marcus Crassus as commander. Trading in confiscated goods, Crassus had made himself rich. Now, using brute force to discipline his new army, he drove the slaves onto the Bruttium Peninsula. Spartacus was killed. Crassus crucified six thousand of the rebel slaves. (Crucifixion, the nailing of a criminal by his hands and feet to a large wooden cross until death, was a common punishment of the era. It would later be used on Jesus of Nazareth. The cross would be taken by Christians as the symbol of their faith in resurrection.)

Leaders of the Populares

In 70 BC, Crassus and Pompey returned to

Bust of Marcus Tullius Cicero, the famous Roman orator

Rome in triumph and in competition for the consulship that year. They agreed to share it. Honored but distrusted by the very Senate Optimates who had appointed them, Crassus and Pompey turned to the opposing party of the people, the Populares. Opposition to Sulla's system combined with Crassus' wealth got them jointly elected.

They repealed much of the Sullan system, including the Senate monopoly on the courts, dividing criminal juries between senators and wealthy nonsenators. They restored power to the tribunes and the censors. The two elected censors, both supporters of Pompey, granted Roman citizenship to the Italian population, enhancing Pompey's popularity. The year marks the end of political control by the Sullan establishment and the beginning of Pompey's dominance.

Pompey bided his time, refusing to take over an ordinary province in 69 BC, the normal route to power. Massive piracy

continued to paralyze trade in the Mediterranean. So little grain reached Rome that starvation threatened. In 67 BC, Pompey was given an extraordinary command with unprecedented power to deal with the issue. Taking over from Marcus Antonius, he gained absolute power at sea. With a fleet of 500 ships, he swept the pirates northeast to Cilicia in just 89 days. There he offered them a choice: give up piracy or fight to the death. He allowed those opting for civilian life to colonize abandoned cities along the coast.

The piracy action put Pompey in the vicinity of Lucullus, who had succeeded in driving Mithridates into Armenia. However, Lucullus had also alienated both Roman businessmen and his own troops with strict policies of honesty and discipline. In 66 BC, out of favor in Rome (where he had a reputation for extravagant banquets) and faced with mutiny, he was forced to cede authority to Pompey. That gave Pompey supreme command in the east. He promptly put it to use defeating Mithridates and arranging for his death.

Pompey spent the next several years reorganizing the east to protect Asia (his greatest source of wealth: he is said to have raised revenues from the provinces by almost 75 percent) with three new provinces

and a circle of clientela (client states). He made Syria a Roman province. He conquered the independent Jewish state surrounding the city of Jerusalem, turning it into a vassal state under a Gentile king in 63 BC. (It is said that when he entered the great temple in Jerusalem as victor, he went only as far as the Jewish high priests would

go, peering through a curtain to see the "Holy of Holies.") In 62 BC, his tasks accomplished, he returned to Rome in glory. Pompey the Great had earned his name by comparison with Alexander the Great.

Crassus, scheming to keep his own power in Rome intact, feared Pompey's return. He also had another opponent in the eloquent lawyer and brilliant orator, Marcus Tullius Cicero.

Cicero

In 70 BC, the year much of Sulla's system was repealed, criminal justice was restored. With it came the rise of Cicero, making his way by political savvy and oratorical ability rather than social class. As *aedile* (or magistrate), Cicero was chosen by the Sicilians to prosecute their corrupt overlord Verres. The case made him famous.

Victorious Roman generals were allowed to enter Rome in triumphal procession at the head of their troops. This is a likeness of a chariot.

731

In addition to their wartime duties, Roman legions were used to build roads. A major example was the Via Appia linking Rome with the south of Italy. The road has been well preserved, as this photograph shows.

Verres had ruled in so exploitive a manner that his subjects had filed a complaint with the Senate. The overlord had counted on his class connections, his wealth, and his presumption that any jury established under Sulla could be bribed. Senate juries, however, were suddenly less corrupt, to the chagrin of the Sicilian. Cicero, playing to the anti-Sulla political mood of the day, presented overwhelming evidence against him in an eloquent speech. Despite the similar class rank of the court, Verres was convicted. This did not stop the exploitation in the provinces; the governors had unlimited power and were expected to take care of their supporters. The large numbers of profit-oriented equites now in the Senate added to the problem. Self-indulgence had replaced the sense of public service once held by the best of the aristocracy. Convictions in extortion cases became unobtainable.

By 63 BC, the situation was ripe for revolution. Cicero believed that the very foundation of the Roman Republic was so shaky, it could be destroyed by a single commander with a strong private army. He contended that the only way to preserve the state was *concordia ordinum* (harmony between the classes), specifically, between the two privileged groups of Roman society, the Optimates (members of the Senate) and the equites (soldiers, traders, and bankers) below them. All over the Italian peninsula, debt and discontent were rampant. Families dispossessed by Sulla wanted restitution. The patrician Lucius Sergius Catalina (Catiline), unable to bribe his way into a consulship, made himself head of a conspiracy to overturn the government in Rome. Cicero, acting as consul, denounced the plot before the Senate, demanding the death penalty for Catiline and his prominent followers.

The young Senator Gaius Julius Caesar argued against execution. Seeking clemency for the conspirators, Caesar entered the public eye for the first time.

As the debate continued, Catiline himself fled to Etruria, only to be killed in battle. The traditionalist Marcus Porcius Cato turned the Senate in Cicero's favor; the remaining conspirators were executed.

Roman roads were built not only for troops who had to cover enormous distances on foot but for all other forms of traffic as well. An example is this merchant with his mule cart, pictured on a floor mosaic in the thermal baths of the Cisiarii family at Ostia.

From Caesar to Augustus

The Rise of Absolute Power

According to ancient legend, the Roman people descended from the Trojan hero Aeneas. He survived the destruction of his own country, it was said, fleeing the ruined city of Troy, with his son Julus to establish the Julian line and a new colony in Latium. This is the subject of much Roman literature, most notably Virgil's epic *The Aeneid*.

Modern archaeological investigation supports the tale, citing evidence from the twelfth century BC. As early as the sixth century BC, the Etruscans, dominant figures on the Latin plain before the Romans,

made mention of Aeneas. They may have handed on the story.

Another legend, elaborated on by the Roman historian Livy in the first century BC, has to do with the origin of the city of Rome itself. Romulus, after whom it was named, interpreted divine omens to mean he was to kill his twin brother Remus and found the new city. (Archaeology, again, lends credence. Evidence has been found that points to the eighth century BC establishment of a Latin village on the Palatine, one of the seven hills of Rome.) Romulus, wrote Livy, was a military leader,

733

Ornamental cup from the Ptolemies' palace in Egypt. Made of layers of semiprecious stone, its varied colors were achieved by cutting out layers.

the first of seven kings ruling Rome from about 754 BC to the beginning of the Republic in 509 BC.

Caesar's Political Rise

Gaius Julius Caesar considered himself the direct descendent of Aeneas and the line of kings. In early 63 BC, he hardly looked the part. He had lost his plea in the Senate for clemency for Catiline and the conspirators who had plotted revolution against Rome. This was a very public failure, one he would subsequently avenge by having Cicero, his senatorial opponent in this case, sent to exile. Although he was a member of the oligarchy (the ruling wealthy) by marriage, he was heavily in debt to Crassus. He had borrowed and spent exorbitant sums, among other things, to gain political office.

Later that year, however, his investment paid off. He managed to get himself elected *pontifex maximus*, head of the largely ceremonial state religion.

This was a significant victory: Caesar had transcended the normal line of political succession, as he had not yet held the office of praetor. Once regarded as the holder of all sacred knowledge, the pontifex maximus had at one time been responsible for the administration of the *jus divinum*, the divine law by which all Rome was run. In 63 BC, maintained by a cynical aristocracy primarily for popular effect, the position still carried great political and social importance. It put Caesar at the top of the aristocracy in a single move and allowed him to dispense virtually unlimited patronage to ensure his power.

Made praetor in 62 BC, he continued his political rise, but debt remained a problem. When he was made governor of southern Spain a year later, Caesar's creditors only let him go after Crassus guaranteed his debts. In Spain, however, Caesar did well, amassing riches from the inhabitants in typical Roman fashion. He returned to Rome in 60 BC more than able to clear all his financial obligations.

Back home, he found that Pompey had made himself a defenseless private citizen. Only two years earlier, Pompey had returned in triumph. The Senate Optimates had given him a great procession – and then asked him to disband his army. The law required this of all victorious commanders who might pose a threat to the Republic. Much to the relief of the Optimates, he had done so. Regardless of his compliance, they continued to view him as a serious menace to their own political control and were now working actively against him. Pompey was learning for the second time that his true allies were not the senators but the plebeians of the peoples' party. (Wealthy plebeians had shared power with the aristocratic patricians since the fourth century.)

The Tripartite Dynasty

Caesar wanted the consulship in 59 BC but lacked the power to gain it on his own. His political opponents raised another issue: a triumphal procession for him. They did not want him garnering the publicity and the popularity a citywide celebration would earn. Caesar yielded to them, choosing to give up the parade in order to run for office. He was elected consul, with the assistance of his old friend Crassus.

Now, as consul, Caesar put together an unlikely alliance. Wanting the money and influence of Crassus and the soldiers' vote that Pompey could still bring in, he managed to unite Crassus and Pompey, themselves enemies, in his support. Marriages, especially Pompey's to Caesar's daughter Julia, reinforced the contract. It was a powerful combination, especially given Caesar's penchant for disregarding any laws he found inconvenient. He simply

The Senate building as it stands today, representing a reconstruction by Diocletian of the one Julius Caesar had constructed at the Forum Romanum in Rome

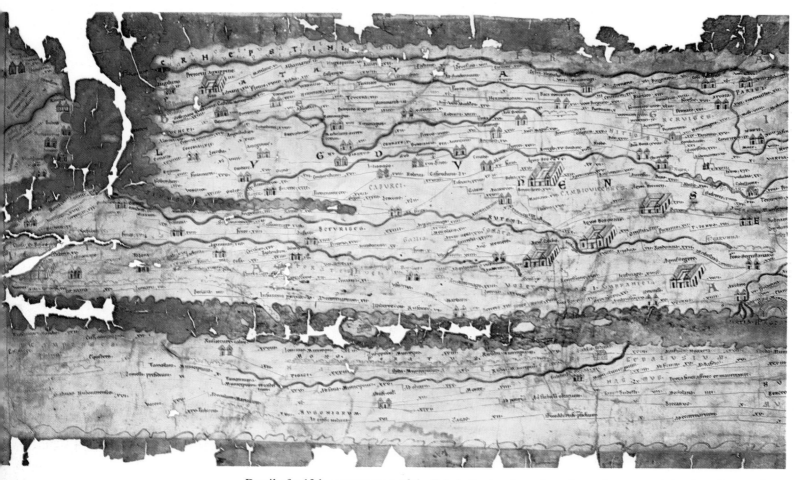

Detail of a 13th-century copy of the Tabula Peutigeriana, the only road map remaining from Roman time

Model of a Roman cargo ship used to transport grain from Egypt. Due to the lack of good navigational instruments and the constant threat of pirates, shipping was very risky.

and Transalpine Gaul. He took an army north. Surprised authorities in Rome began to receive messages, many from Caesar himself, about an undeclared war winning new territory for the Republic. Caesar later collected his reports into a single volume called *De Bello Gallico* (On Gallic War). Gradually, Pompey and Crassus grew concerned about Caesar's success and his rapidly growing power. The Senate Optimates felt likewise.

In 58 BC, the patrician Publius Clodius Pulcher, acting as tribune, went after the aging lawyer Cicero on behalf of Caesar. A fanatical member of the Populares, Publius had assumed the position of a plebeian, replacing his aristocratic name Claudius with the unpretentious Clodius. A fiery public speaker, he used a private army to intimidate those not impressed by his words alone. The issue he raised against Cicero was an old one: the execution of Catiline and his fellow conspirators in 63 BC. Accusing Cicero of the summary execution of Roman citizens, he drove the lawyer into exile.

By 57 BC, the tripartite dynasty began to disintegrate. Pompey arranged for Cicero's return. The lawyer, loyal to tradition and the Senate, tried to further the breakup by

employed force as he chose. It soon became obvious that the alliance, not the Senate, ruled Rome.

By 58 BC, Caesar had arranged a special command for himself, the governorship of the provinces of Illyria, Cisalpine Gaul,

wooing Pompey to the Senate side. He almost succeeded.

The Fall of the Tripartite Dynasty

Relations among the three members of the alliance grew increasingly worse. Caesar was required to make a secret trip in 56 BC to Luca (on the Italian peninsula) to negotiate another contract.

In 55 BC, while Pompey and Crassus were sharing the consulship, details of the secret agreement came to light. The revived pact featured a three-way monopoly of military power. There had been a movement to get Caesar recalled from Gaul. Now it appeared he would remain in Gaul another five years. Upon his return, he would be guaranteed both another consulship and continued army command. Crassus was made governor of the new province of Syria and equipped with a sizable army to bring the Parthians there under control. Pompey was made commander of Spain but would stay near Rome to carry on the consular administration, delegating his authority in Spain to others. Crassus would continue nominal joint service with him as consul.

Rome was forced to submit to the arrangement. Even the traditionalist Cicero acquiesced to the point of taking on responsibility as spokesman of the alliance. The old oligarchy he had believed in, with its adherence to a rule of law and its system of patrician-dominated government, had failed him. No one really agreed with him now. Ultimately, he would stay with Pompey all the way to the final defeat at Pharsalus.

Crassus took his army to Syria in search of a victory that might let him equal the power of his allies. In 53 BC, he crossed the Euphrates River with 40,000 infantry, only to meet the arrows of 10,000 Parthian cavalry fired from a distance that rendered any foot soldiers useless. Fleeing into the desert, the Roman troops were trapped at Carrhae and slaughtered. Crassus escaped with a few survivors and subsequently attempted to negotiate with the Parthians. They agreed to discussion but, when he arrived at the appointed place, they murdered him.

Now only Caesar and Pompey were left. Julia had died in 54 BC, weakening the ties between. Caesar's complete conquest of Gaul had given him prestige and wealth almost equal to Pompey's. He used it, as Pompey did not, to influence friends and to buy support. The powerful allies had little common interest.

Meanwhile, chaos reigned in Rome. Gangs terrorized the city, especially the private troopers of Clodius, unmatched by any government force. Pompey could have taken over with his private army, but the Senate was reluctant to grant him the power. Only Milo, a supporter of the Optimates, opposed Clodius with his own client army. In January, 52 BC, Milo's men killed

Clodius in a minor gang battle along the Via Appia. It was impossible to hold praetor elections as scheduled because of the street riots that resulted.

Later that year, Pompey offered the official Roman government his assistance in return for legitimization. He sought both the actual administration and the respectability it provided. The state, in turn, led by Marcus Porcius Cato, long-term opponent of Caesar, recognized the value of Pompey's protection.

Marble portrait of Queen Cleopatra of Egypt, the last ruler of the Ptolemaic dynasty

De Bello Gallico (On Gallic War)

Caesar summarized the periodic reports he sent to Rome on his military expeditions in Gaul into one large work, *De Bello Gallico* (or On Gallic War). A lively and clear account of his actions in Gaul, it also provides extensive information about the inhabitants. However, it cannot be said to constitute objective history; Caesar wrote it to defend his policy to Rome. His intent was to maximize his achievements and to increase his reputation in Rome.

Caesar had originally moved to Gaul with the intention of setting up a power base in the north. He assumed it would provide him with a faithful army, raised in part from the local people he conquered. Between the mountain ranges of the Pyrenees and the Alps lay the highly Romanized province of Transalpine Gaul. Several of the vying groups in the region sought Caesar's support in their struggles. He and his legions rapidly obliged, subjugating peoples all the way to the Rhine.

By the time Caesar established the Rhine as the northern border of the Roman Republic, it became clear to the squabbling Gauls that they had invited an unwelcome and hungry guest. He had a bridge built across the Rhine to let the Germans know his legions could reach them in their home territory, as well. He consolidated his victory over the Gauls only with considerable difficulty. Rebellions were frequent; the need to subdue them almost constant. He was forced to cross to Britain twice to intimidate the Gauls there.

Statue of
a Gallic soldier
wearing a metal tunic
and armed
with a shield

Pompey saw Milo, with the power he had gained in the streets of Rome, as a potential rival. Fearing that the Senate might come to consider Milo an alternative to himself, Pompey asked for a decision on the question. The Senate opted for Pompey, appointing him sole consul to restore order. Pompey at once went after Milo, getting him convicted.

Pompey, who had recently completed a marriage alliance with the noble Quintus Metellus Scipio, now arranged for him to share the consulship. He meant this as indication of the legitimacy of his own intentions.

Crossing the Rubicon
Caesar, in isolated opposition to both

Bust of Gaius Julius Caesar as victor, crowned with the traditional laurel wreath

Silver dish
with a portrait of Queen
Cleopatra

voted, declaring Caesar an outlaw. With his army on the banks of the Rubicon, the river border between Cisalpine Gaul and Italy, Caesar reviewed the situation, ultimately deciding to seize the initiative. The next day, crossing the Rubicon (an expression that today still carries a connotation of decisive action), he took his army on a fast march to Rome to take power.

Pompey promptly fled first Rome and then all Italy, as more and more cities fell to Caesar. His plan had been to contain Caesar in Italy, but his intended victim had other ideas. In another lightning move, Caesar captured Massilia and Spain from Pompey's generals and went on to Greece. In 48 BC, he entered Thessalonika in Pompey's wake.

Disgusted senators persuaded Pompey to stand and fight, to no avail. Within a few hours, Caesar defeated his troops near the city of Pharsalus. Pompey himself escaped to Egypt, where he was killed by a lone assassin trying to ingratiate himself with Caesar, an ignoble death. Caesar had followed. In Alexandria, the Egyptians offered him Pompey's head on a platter. He could not look at it.

Pompey and the state, bargained over the next two years for his political future and his personal safety. Behind the scenes, Pompey worked for Caesar's recall, whose term in Gaul was almost over in any case. In 49 BC, Pompey finally voiced his opposition to Caesar openly. The Senate

Marcus Junius Brutus, one-time friend of Julius Caesar and also one of his assassins

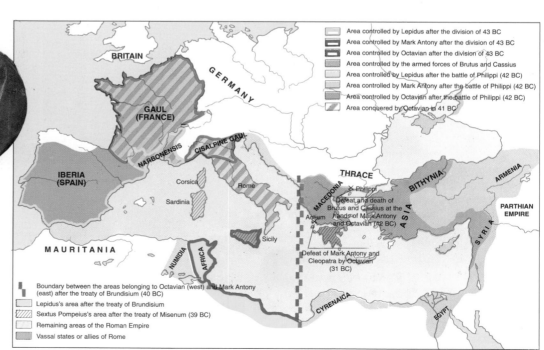

Map depicting the political situation on the Mediterranean Sea during the civil wars which broke out after the assassination of Julius Caesar (44–30 BC)

He was, however, quite able to look at Cleopatra, young, beautiful, and intelligent, the last of Ptolemy's royal line. She may have seduced Caesar out of opportunism, but while civil war raged outside the palace, the famous romance blossomed within. Caesar, narrowly escaping a plot to kill him, installed her on the throne of Alexandria and defended her position against her younger brother. Just 13 at the time, the boy had been put forward as claimant to the throne. In the series of fights that followed, the young pretender was killed; his party was eliminated. Meanwhile, Cleopatra gave birth to a son, Caesarion.

Caesar's battles were not yet over. Loyalists and local native troops Pompey had recruited held on in the province of Africa, Cato among them, until 46 BC. Caesar led his forces to Thapsus, where he destroyed them. Cato, rejecting the pardon Caesar granted him, killed himself, leaving Caesar as absolute ruler of the Roman Republic.

Caesar's Administration

Back in Rome, Caesar tried to establish a legal basis for the power he already had. With the help of a compliant Senate, he had himself made both consul and dictator. Under Roman law, dictatorial authority could be granted to a consul or to anyone designated by a consul. While the new ruling gave him virtually limitless authority, Caesar's real power depended on his soldiers and his military prowess.

Many of those who believed in Caesar became disappointed in his administration. Despite his vast power, he neither planned nor carried out any of the real reform the Republic demanded. The domestic situation was little different from what it had been in the chaos of 52 BC.

To gain control, Caesar increased the number and the severity of legal penalties. He installed several hundred supporters in the Senate, increased the number of senators and magistrates, and generously handed out citizenship with its attendant privileges. While he cut back grain handouts to the poor, on the grounds that they were being misused, Caesar also started a massive drive toward colonization, renovating devastated cities, and giving tens of thousands of people new homes all over the Republic.

People had expected large scale cancellation of debts and redistribution of property. Caesar did confiscate the holdings of some of his enemies but he pardoned most and seized nothing. He wanted popularity, not the persecution of his former enemies. He had the statue of Pompey put back in the Senate after his own overzealous admirers had pulled it down. Pompey, he felt, had been a worthy opponent. He expressed public regret, as well, that a man like Cato had committed suicide rather than accept his pardon.

Bust of Mark Antony. After Caesar's death, he became Queen Cleopatra's lover, joining battle with her against Rome.

Marcus Vipsanius Agrippa, friend and general of Octavian, who won the battle of Actium

Despite the honors heaped on him by the fawning Senate, Caesar appeared to reject the concept of kingship, something detested in the Republic. (At the *lupercalia*, a great festival for the people, his lieutenant Mark Antony offered him a golden coronet, ancient symbol of a king's power. The watching audience disapproved. Caesar refused to accept it, leading to speculation as to whether the whole scene had been staged to make his rejection of kingship clear – or whether public disapproval had put him off at the last moment.)

Caesar's most important contribution may have been the calendar. The Romans had originally had a 355-day year with an extra month every other year, set by the pontifex maximus. Caesar, while holding this office, had Alexandrian scholars fix the length of the year at exactly 365 1/4 days, introducing a new calendar with years of 365 days and an extra day (the 29th of February) every four years to make up the difference. (This date was a logical choice since the Romans originally celebrated the new year on the first of March.) This Julian calendar survived intact until the sixteenth century.

The Ides of March, 44 BC

Under Caesar's calendar, the fifteenth day of March, May, July, and October was called the ides. In 44 BC, the ides of March would prove to be a turning point in history.

The previous year, Caesar had been forced to go to Spain to put down a major rebellion instituted by Pompey's sons. At the battle of Munda, said to be the worst in all his wars, Caesar succeeded in eliminating the last of Pompey's supporters.

Caesar returned to Rome more powerful than ever, only to face a conspiracy of some 60 men, organized by Brutus and Cassius. He was stabbed to death on the Senate floor March 15, 44 BC.

The body of Caesar lay at the foot of Pompey's statue. Panic filled the Senate. The plotters themselves panicked, wandering the city with bloody daggers. Only Mark Antony kept his wits about him. Named by Caesar as executor of his will, he set about his task before an immense crowd assembled in front of the Senate. He laid the blood-stained body of Caesar on a bier, named the murderers, and read out Caesar's will.

The dictator, it turned out, had left his gardens to the state and a moderate amount of money (300 *sesterces*) to every citizen. The crowd went into a frenzy of adoration, building a huge funeral pyre for Caesar. From the flames which flared up high around the body, they lit torches to set fire to the houses of the plotters. Power in Rome would fall to Antony.

Octavian

An unexpected challenger presented himself in the person of Caesar's nephew and

A Roman war galley from about 35 BC. The ship was primarily powered by oarsmen. Equipped with a catapult which could be fired, it also had a tower from which archers could shoot.

adopted son and heir, Octavian. Not yet 20, he proved to be a formidable political opponent. He commanded loyalty from Caesar's old party, part of which left Antony for him. He also cooperated with the Senate, finding a further ally in Cicero. Now a prominent voice in the Senate, Cicero delivered a series of orations against Antony, presenting him as an enemy of ancient Roman freedoms.

By 43 BC, Cassius and Brutus had taken control of the eastern provinces and the military. Octavian joined battle with the incumbent consuls to defeat Antony at Mutina. Victory seemed inevitable until the two old consuls died. Octavian acquired their consulship mantle by force. He then joined Lepidus (the most prominent Caesarian with an army) and Antony himself to form the *triumviri rei publicae constituendae* (the trio for settling the constitution). They would, indeed, reconstruct the state as the first Triumvirate.

The Triumvirate
Antony sealed his compact with Octavian by marrying his sister Octavia. The new Triumvirate issued banishment lists, as had been done by Sulla. Used to dispossess opponents, they allowed the Triumvirate to seize a victim's property and put him to death. An early victim was old Cicero, now denounced. His execution was pushed through by Antony.

In 42 BC, the Triumvirate defeated and killed Brutus and Cassius, dividing the world as they knew it. Octavian received the west, Antony the east, while Lepidus had to make do with Africa. The only problem was now at sea: Pompey's son Sextus still had a powerful fleet.

In 36 BC, Octavian defeated Sextus near the island of Sicily. Lepidus had failed in an attempt to take over that island. Octavian took Africa away from him and banished him to a small town on the Italian peninsula. The Triumvirate had dwindled to Octavian and Antony.

Antony and Cleopatra
The leaders set out on separate campaigns, Antony to Egypt, where he married the forty-year-old Cleopatra and sought to establish Alexandria as his base of operations. Declaring Cleopatra "Queen of queens" and her son Caesarion "King of kings," he made his own sons by Cleopatra kings in various regions in Asia.

In Rome, Octavian used this in a propaganda campaign against Antony. He claimed

In the 18th century, the painter Georg Platzer reconstructed the battle of Actium (31 BC). Mark Antony stands in the middle of the galley with his sword drawn, Cleopatra is on the right.

743

Antony was betraying Roman interests. Public opinion, especially among the Roman upper class, was increasingly on Octavian's side. A year later the Triumvirate would be officially terminated.

Actium

Antony and Cleopatra prepared for war, equipping a colossal fleet of over five hundred ships in the Aegean Sea. They sailed into the Adriatic. In 31 BC, the Roman fleet under Agrippa forced Antony's ships to combat near Actium, on the west coast of Greece. It was a disgrace for Antony. Shortly into battle, Cleopatra left the fleet in her flagship; Antony followed. When his army heard how he had run away, they gave up without a fight.

Octavian pursued his opponents slowly, arriving in Alexandria the following year. Antony killed himself. Cleopatra tried out her seductive talents once more, this time on Octavian. He declined, insisting she ac-

company his triumphal procession through Rome. Cleopatra chose to die by snake bite (from an asp) rather than suffer this disgrace. Octavian killed both Caesarion and Antony's oldest son by Cleopatra, leaving him with nothing more to fear. The triumphal celebration in Rome lasted three days.

Relief in stone showing the victory at Actium: Octavian the victor rides the waves, trampling Antony underfoot.

One of the reliefs of the *Ara Pacis Augustae* (Altar of the Peace of Augustus). The Roman Senate had this altar erected at the Campus Martius, after the triumphal return of Emperor Augustus from Spain. Members of the imperial family can be seen on the relief. Livia, Augustus's wife, is on the left.

Dictatorship

The Principate in Rome

In 30 BC, after the suicides of Antony and Cleopatra, Octavian was unquestioned master of the Roman world. Sustained by the vast wealth of the annexed Egypt, he would remain so for the next 40 years, the first Roman emperor. The form of government he established in the new Roman Empire, the Principate (from his title Princeps), would remain essentially unchanged for the next 200 years.

Octavian's world required a restoration of law and order, a government to override the turmoil of aristocratic intrigue and individual ambition. He had more than sufficient military power to enforce order but he sought to legitimize his power by making use of traditional government practice. He did this initially by carrying out the first Roman census since 70 BC. This enabled Octavian to establish new electoral rolls and to use his influence to get himself elected consul. The office made him the

The remains of the *Mars Ultor* (Mars the Avenger) Temple in the Forum of Augustus in Rome. This temple was erected by Augustus in memory of the punishment of Julius Caesar's assassins.

civilian head of government. Octavian would be reelected continually until 23 BC.

Octavian's Titles

In contrast to what was often said of Caesar, he did not seek the crown. In 27 BC, Octavian nominally relinquished the extraordinary powers he had assumed, declaring that he was returning them to the Senate and the Roman people (Senatus Populusque Romanus). How little this actually meant was indicated by the reaction of the Senate: it promptly gave Octavian the honorary title Augustus (sublime).

He already bore the title *Imperator* (commander in chief). He used both, so that, in practice, Augustus replaced Octavian. In the east, the people changed imperator into *autocrator* (or dictator). The last term was perhaps the best indicator of

his position; Augustus did not actually plan to give up power.

He and his successors put great value on their descent from Caesar. That this descent was by adoption gave even more reason to stress the name. It meant that succession was a matter of choice, not an accident of birth. Hence, over the years, Caesar came to be used as a title of address. (This would continue all over Europe. Medieval kings would have themselves crowned Caesar, later altered to Kaiser, Keizer, or Czar.) Octavian thus came to be called Caesar Augustus.

Another title also came to be used for him: princeps (prince or first citizen of Rome). He preferred it because of the connotation of legitimacy it offered. He presented himself as the first servant of the empire, in keeping with the long-standing Roman tradition of public service. Despite his preponderance of military power, he liked the trappings of civilian authority. What distinguished his reign is the fact that he held several civilian offices, simultaneously and without time limit, that had once been held by a number of individuals for limited terms.

The Senate

In 28 BC, Augustus also became *princeps senatus*, the first or leading member of the Senate, the body from which his imperial power nominally came. Augustus considered the Senate the embodiment of Roman tradition and public opinion, although it lacked any genuine power while he was emperor. It issued binding decrees, functioned as the court of last appeal, and ostensibly monitored government finances. Augustus actually controlled them. In fact, Augustus controlled the very membership of the Senate. No senator served without his approval.

He purged the body of those he considered unworthy, allowing sons of senators, reputable army veterans of sufficient

Statue of Augustus as general and leader of his army. The statue was found in the villa of his wife Livia at Prima Porta. In his left hand, he carries a general's staff. At his feet is an *amoretto* (cupid) on a dolphin.

wealth, and certain minor magistrates (the *vigintivirate*) election to the Senate's lowest rank of quaestor. The position, like the magistracies above it (aedile and praetor), was unpaid. Yet respectful of public reaction, Augustus consistently maintained cordial relations with the

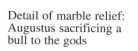

Detail of marble relief: Augustus sacrificing a bull to the gods

747

Senate and carried on an appearance of consultation with it.

In keeping with his penchant for tradition, Augustus tried to mold a patrician elite, powerful, incorruptible, and loyal to him. The remaining Optimate families should have formed the ideal core of this elite, but he found their circle too small and too corrupt. His purging of the Senate did not help his number problem. He needed fresh blood. There was no alternative but to advance the equites (members of the rank below that of senator).

The Equites

The typical individual (the *eques*) of this lower order might begin as an army officer and rise through the ranks of what became a civil service under Augustus. He expanded the equestrian order to include Roman citizens of decent reputation and adequate wealth, regardless of their rank at birth. The revised order offered profitable careers to thousands and developed into a major social institution. Equites would go on to fill responsible posts all over the empire.

Augustus raised a number of prominent equites to senatorial rank, at the same time initiating a policy that gave all incumbent senators new status. He also established a minimum income requirement for holding senatorial office (a million sesterces); if his new senators were no longer required to be of proper rank at birth, at least they would be of adequate means.

The Provinces

The Senate itself was given new tasks, charged with the day-to-day running of Rome, of the rest of the Italian peninsula, and of several provinces (referred to as "public"). These held little strategic importance. Senators who served as governors in those outlying provinces were selected by lot for one-year terms and were allowed no legions.

Augustus retained personal control of all other provinces (hence called "imperial"). He alone appointed their governors who served exclusively at his pleasure rather than for set time periods. Most of these regions were militarily important. Equites, rather than senators, were occasionally permitted governorships in the imperial provinces.

Most important of these was Egypt, with its Ptolemic treasures and its grain. With the exception of Egypt, no equestrian provinces were permitted troops. (Pontius Pilate was the equestrian governor of the province of Judea at the time of the crucifixion of Christ.)

Within each province, whether imperial or senatorial, were the *civitates* (self-governing autonomous communities) through which the emperor actually directed affairs. As they grew increasingly Latinized, their status changed to *municipia* (municipal towns, whose townspeople were accorded Roman citizenship). The civitates paid tribute, as did all provinces. This money went for military protection, the burgeoning civil service, and the extensive public works' efforts of the emperor.

Augustus favored the province and the inhabitants of Italy, where he was born. Under him, the Roman citizens of his native region found new spirit, prosperity, and pride. He fostered that with the con-

Livia, wife of Augustus, portrayed as a priestess, one of her many official functions

748

The ruins of Livia's palace, home of Augustus and his wife, near the Forum Romanum on the Palatine in Rome

struction of monuments, aqueducts, and highways, particularly in Rome.

The New Rome

Despite its great number of inhabitants, Rome still had the look of an old walled *oppidum* (or fortified town) grown beyond its boundaries. The public buildings were in a state of disrepair. The city was crowded and dirty. Even the Forum, center of Roman public life, was too small. Augustus set about giving Rome the outward splendor he required.

"I found a city of stone, and I will leave behind a city of marble," he boasted, and did so. He had marble temples built in the center of town and replaced the old forum with another one nearby. (This set a prece-

dent for later emperors who each in succession added a forum to the center of Rome.) He had the access roads to the city improved and the River Tiber dredged, but behind all the improvement still lay the slums where the great mass of the people lived. Little is left of that aspect of Rome; today's tourists see only the skeleton of the emperor's ostentation.

Augustus also moved to protect the people of Rome against famine. In the past, a foreign enemy needed only to control the sea to starve out Rome. Augustus established an administration to maintain grain supply and organized annual grain imports from Egypt. He used grain distribution to the masses to improve his own popularity.

Portrait head of Drusus, Livia's son from her earlier marriage to Tiberius Claudius Nero. Drusus successfully led the Roman army into Germany, as far as the river Elbe. He was killed in a fall from his horse.

749

The Gemma Augustea cameo celebrating the victory of Tiberius over the Germans in 7 AD. Tiberius, in the top left-hand corner, is stepping from his war chariot. In the middle, the Emperor Augustus is being crowned, while various gods look on. At the bottom is the battlefield after the battle: Roman soldiers have taken German prisoners and are erecting a victory banner.

Cultural Life

Peace and the new prosperity gave literature the chance to blossom as never before. Augustus understood the need for a Roman literature to make traditional ideals come alive. He welcomed authors, as did his friend Maecenas, noted patron of the arts. Some of their clients (Virgil as great heroic poet; Horace as witty cultural pundit, he was noted for his epigrams; and Livy as historian) claim lasting places in world literature.

One of them fell into disgrace: the poet Ovid. During the chastity drive, Augustus banished him to Tomi on the Black Sea for publishing erotic poetry and becoming involved in a scandal with Julia, his own daughter. Ovid's poetic imagination continued to flourish in exile. He wrote flattering verses to Augustus in the vain hope of reinstatement to his beloved Rome. He would die in Tomi.

Domestic Policy

Augustus found himself with an exhausted empire, its economy and its cities in ruin, its people tired of urban riots and wandering bands of robbers and revolutionaries.

The death struggle of the Republic had also taken a toll among the Optimates. Famous old patrician families had died out, traditional values were ignored, and even the religious rites had become confused.

Caesar Augustus attempted to deal with all of these problems.

Police Services

The people of the slums in Rome were frequent victims of vying gangs. The alleys gave them ample place to hide. The people were also prone to riot themselves during the final days of the Republic. Augustus formed four cohorts of special troops to maintain order. Their leader, the *praefectus urbi* (prefect of the city), became one of the most powerful men in Rome. This trained riot police appear to have been effective, although serious riots flared occasionally. Augustus also appointed 7,000 night watchmen to watch for fires and crime after dark, led by a *praefectus vigilum* (prefect of the watchers). While neither effort made Rome completely safe, improvement was significant.

Traditional Family Values

Augustus set about the restoration of family tradition. He proclaimed chastity laws to strengthen what he saw as slack

Gaius Cilnius Maecenas, a friend of Augustus, noted for his patronage of the arts and literature.

morality. Viewing the ideal family as father, mother, and as many children as possible, he established a *lex iulia* conferring privileges on those with children and imposing civil restrictions on single people and the childless.

Other laws made marriage easier (even if the parents of the bride and bridegroom objected) and divorce harder. Illicit lovers faced banishment, property confiscation, and a ban on all future marriage. The measures, intended to provide Rome with the citizens needed to maintain its position, were of little use.

Augustus did not consider himself subject to his own laws. He was married three times, the second time to an older woman previously married to two consuls, with a child by each. Augustus divorced his second wife for Livia, then the wife of the

The Romans left their influence on the landscape all over Europe. This aqueduct, built in Augustan times, can still be seen in Segovia, Spain.

A Roman cameo with a portrait of the Emperor Augustus. The jewels were added in the Middle Ages.

Damaged portrait of Virgil (Publius Vergilius Maro), one of the great poets of the Augustan era. He wrote the famous Roman epic *The Aeneid*.

elderly Tiberius Claudius Nero who agreed to a divorce.

Augustus brought up his daughter Julia (by his second wife) and his granddaughter of the same name very strictly, requiring daily reports on them. Once they were out of his control, their promiscuous behavior was talked about all over Rome. Augustus eventually banished them from the city and, according to the historian Suetonius, hid himself from the people out of shame for a time.

Religion

To most Romans in the Augustan era, religion was more of an outdated concept than anything else. Ancient Romans had adopted classical Hellenistic mythology with its hierarchy of gods, each with a clearly defined task and personality. The Greeks contended that the souls of the dead lived on in the vicinity of the grave. The Romans believed that besides the soul (or *anima*, a word which literally means breath or wind), something else remained after death, namely the *umbra* (or shadow). At death, the shadows departed into the underworld through cracks in the earth.

Charon, the ferryman, rowed them across the River of the Dead, the Styx, to be judged. Those condemned were thrown into the Tartatus for punishment. Those saved were allowed to enter the blossoming valleys of the Elysian Fields. These shadows of the dead made up the large swarm of *manes* (a word always used in the plural).

The manes could assist their earthly families, appearing in dreams and revelations to advise, but could also turn against them. Those who offended the manes would have evil spirits to deal with.

Augustus was familiar with other philosophic ideas of the time, as well, like the cults of Isis and Christianity. The poet Ovid claimed that the blessed replicated their earthly ways of life there. On the epitaph of a slave it is written that he is working in the underworld, just as he did on earth. Virgil told of the shadows of blessed ones who amused themselves by singing, talking about their weapons, and holding chariot races. Epitaphs, texts, and monuments reveal both skepticism about the immortality of the soul and the great popularity of the new-found religions.

Augustus revived festivals (probably of Etruscan origin) supposed to appease evil spirits. Once scheduled every 10 years, but last held in 49 BC, they had been postponed by war between Caesar and Pompey. In 17 BC, Augustus revitalized them to celebrate Rome's greatness. Sporting events by day alternated with feasts and processions by night. The intent was both restoration of tradition and prophecy of a prosperous future. The poet Horace composed a *Carmen Saeculare* (centenary celebration hymn) to mark the beginning of the new era.

The emperor met personally with the priests of all the Roman colleges to revitalize religious practice. Once, it had been commonplace to invoke the gods in public life. Carefully prescribed prayers and actions could affect the *numina* (external spiritual powers) favorably or unfavorably. The appearance of piety could still have propaganda benefit and enhance the emperor's prestige and popularity. Augustus replaced crumbling temples with Hellenistic buildings and raised the great rectangular Pantheon (typical of the Republican era) to all gods, as its name

Fresco from a house at Pompeii, with a scene from the epic poem, *The Aeneid*. Its principal character Aeneas
was the hero of Troy and the legendary founder of Rome. He is seen here being treated for a thigh wound. The goddess Venus,
his protector and patroness, looks on.

implied. He did not neglect his own reputation in this regard. (The round Pantheon seen today is the later work of Hadrian who reoriented the temple 180° and incorporated the Augustan temple into the new portico.)

Deification

In the eastern cities, it was not uncommon to deify rulers, worshipping them as gods. It was no surprise that cults would originate there to worship Augustus. He did nothing to stop the practice, as it could only reinforce his authority. (It was not altogether out of keeping with ancient Roman tradition. In the monarchy that predated the Republic of Rome, kings were considered to hold religious authority as well as military, legal, and political. That religious authority was handed over to the *rex sacrorum*, a priest given lifelong appointment, during the republic.)

Worship of Augustus caught on in the towns along the Italian peninsula. Special colleges were formed for the purpose. Their priests (called *augustales*) were generally freed slaves who could make a career of this official worship. While the custom was not formally introduced in Rome, Augustus did build a shrine in every neighborhood devoted to his guardian spirit. The cult of the Princeps entered Rome through the back door.

Pax Augusta

One of the many themes of Augustus's propaganda was himself as peace lover. He had a great "altar of peace," the *ara pacis*, constructed in the north of the city. Its reliefs show him offering traditional sacrifices to peace. In reality, his reputation here rests mainly on caution. Augustus never went into battle himself. He had reliable generals take care of that for him. The late Crassus, who died in defeat at the hands of the Parthians, had shown him how major expeditions might end.

The personal allegiance of his army was vital to Augustus. Every January 1, every soldier swore an oath of loyalty to him (or whatever successor he might eventually choose). The emperor's adoptive father,

The Forum Romanum was the political and cultural center of the city of Rome and the entire Roman Empire. Here the temples of the main gods were erected. The Senate held its meetings in the Curia. The state archives were kept in the Tabularium. This reconstruction drawing shows the Forum in the heyday of the Empire.

Julius Caesar (actually his uncle), had been deified. The support pledged by his soldiers to that name carried the weight of a religious vow.

To allay popular fear of a large military, Augustus had demobilized his army after the battle at Actium in 30 BC, reducing the number of legions from 60 to 28. It now constituted a permanent standing army of 300,000. (Augustus also maintained a large bodyguard, the praetorian cohorts, and a marine corps on the imperial fleet.) The army was comprised of two corps, the legionnaires (Roman citizens from municipal towns) and their supporting ranks, the auxiliaries (from tribal regions, made Roman citizens upon retirement from service). Within the legions, the officers were all Roman citizens. However, birth caste played a part. The top ranks (*legati* and *tribuni*) were senators or at least equites. Below them were centuriones who typically entered from the municipal towns of Italy.

The army was a factor in the consolidation of the empire aside from any question of military conquest. Widespread Roman encampments were created to maintain a military presence throughout the empire. Designed for protection of one life style, they in fact frequently developed into permanent societies of their own. Over centuries, many grew into major European cities.

Although it was illegal for soldiers to marry, many had children, often granted Roman citizenship. Retiring soldiers frequently settled in the regions where they had been assigned. Augustus encouraged this, granting free land to such military men to form highly regarded colonies.

Roman Territory

Augustus gained territory slowly. It took years of fighting to subdue the last tribes in Spain. Victory was sealed with the establishment of several colonies. The city of Caesar augusta (Saragossa) emerged from one of these, its original alpine people subjugated in a cruel and genocidal war.

Roman power spread to the Danube River in the Balkans, the energy and cruelty of Augustan generals yielding two new provinces, Moesia and Pannonia. During the Balkan Wars, other generals extended Roman influence to the banks of the Elbe in an effort to force the Germanic people to leave their Gallic neighbors in peace. Control of German peoples between the Rhine and the Elbe was, however, quite superficial.

When the Viceroy Varus tried to tighten his grip, the Germans united against him. Varus entered the virgin forests and marshes of Germany with three legions. By 9 BC, the Germans, led by Arminius, had destroyed them. Only a few soldiers made it back to the Rhine to break the news. (Augustus is said to have cried over and over again, "Varus, Varus, give me back my legions!") That defeat apparently convinced him it was better to consolidate power in areas already conquered than to extend it. That the Romans made no further serious attempts to expand beyond the Rhine is still evident in the language and way of life of the people along that river.

Meanwhile, as usual, the Parthians threatened in the east. As Augustus consolidated his possessions in Syria and Asia Minor,

both the Romans and the Parthians kept the civil war in Armenia going, supporting different pretenders to the throne. The Romans sided with what proved to be the weaker party, which was hated by the common people, and lost.

Augustus negotiated (rather than fought for) the return of the regimental colors captured by the Parthians from Crassus in 53 BC. This fact was used to illustrate his love of peace.

Augustus contended that previous conquests already offered sufficient protection for the empire against invasion. He saw no reason to attempt others. Except for Britannia, where genuinely expansionist policies were pursued, nothing would be added to the empire for a century.

The Forum Romanum was excavated by archeologists in the 19th century. This photograph shows the Forum as it is now. We can recognize a number of buildings from the reconstruction drawing on the previous page.

Successors

Eventually, his regularly recurring illnesses reminded Augustus that he had to think about his successor. Augustus himself had no son to inherit the empire. He had originally considered his classmate and son-in-law, Marcus Vipsanius Agrippa, for the task, but Agrippa died a year after his appointment.

Both Agrippa's widow Julia, daughter of the emperor, and the succession itself shifted to Tiberius, a son of Livia by her first husband. Augustus, outraged at Julia's actions, forced Tiberius to cast her off. Tiberius did so resentfully and subsequently retreated to isolation on the island of Rhodes. The experience seems to have turned him into the mistrustful pessimist he eventually was as princeps.

Augustus then turned to his grandsons, the children of Julia and Agrippa. He adopted them, which gave them the name Caesar. Both boys appeared to show great promise, but died young.

Ultimately, Augustus was left with Tiberius as his only option. He arranged what proved to be an uncomfortable reconciliation with his stepson. Tiberius returned from Rhodes to be adopted by Augustus in 4 AD. By 13 AD, he had been confirmed in various governmental roles and gradually handed control of the empire. By the time Augustus died in 14 AD, Tiberius was able to take over completely with no opposition.

Maintaining Roman territory continued to be the new emperor's top priority, as it would be for most emperors after him. Roughly speaking, the Augustan borders would hold for four centuries.

The Emperor Augustus, pictured as legislator, dressed in a toga and holding a scroll

Roman mosaic showing stage actors prepare for a performance in their dressing room. On the right, an actor puts on his costume. On the left, a musician practices his double flute. In the middle, stage masks lie in a basket ready for the show.

The First Emperors

The Rule of the Julio-Claudian Dynasty

Upon the death of Caesar Augustus, the Senate deified him, as it had his predecessor, in keeping with the long-standing Roman tradition of honoring great leaders in this manner. Tiberius, adopted by Augustus and groomed as heir apparent, would have a hard time matching the political craftsmanship of this "god."

Tiberius was the first of four related successors to gain the emperorship despite the

Bust of Drusus, Tiberius's son from his first marriage. Extremely popular, Drusus was eventually murdered by his wife Livilla, at the instigation of Sejanus.

fact that no inherited right of succession existed. Augustus and the four together comprise what is known as the Julio-Claudian dynasty. Related to Augustus through blood lines or marriage, these were Tiberius, Gaius (called Caligula), Claudius I, and Nero. The issue was larger than simply the order of inheritance; it had to do, as well, with the factor of ability. Ideally, each new princeps would be not just the heir apparent but one ready to assume the mantle. No legal right of succession had been established under the constitution. Augustus had not altered the constitution. He had simply established his own position of power within its old structures. But if the principate he had fashioned were to continue, each princeps needed to be able to designate his own successor in sufficient time to prepare him well. Augustus made Tiberius co-ruler before his own death in an effort to guarantee continued able imperial leadership.

The concept of succession became a tradition of the Roman Empire. Each emperor sought a suitable candidate during his lifetime, usually a member of the family who would then be adopted as a son. The Senate still provided an official sanction after succession became more or less dynastic. Because no law established what relative had a right to be emperor or in what order, the consequences were fatal. Any ambitious person with enough influence might aspire to be emperor. If it could not be done with popular consent, then it would have to be done without it. Few emperors died a natural death. Fewer still lived without fear of plots from among the phi-losophers, scoundrels, counselors, freed slaves, favorites, and administrators surrounding him. The atmosphere at court was permeated with intrigue. While a career as a public servant offered unprecedented opportunity, it also presented unprecedented danger.

Tiberius (Emperor: AD 14–37)

It was under this emperor that Jesus Christ was crucified. Crucifixion (the nailing of the victim to a wooden cross until he died) was a common means of executing criminals at the time.

Tiberius came to power an austere and bitter man. He had lived his life in the shadow of his stepfather, the emperor, his happiness ruined by a forced marriage to a woman he despised. Moody and unpopular, he proved to be a meticulous administrator, thrifty to the point of stinginess, cutting back on public expense. This did not improve his popularity with the Roman people. The masses had expected spectacular events and overflowing grain handouts from their emperor.

Unlucky with his contemporary historians, Tiberius was described for centuries as an unapproachable ruler who despised his subjects. (We rely here primarily on Cornelius Tacitus, who made no secret of his republican ideas, and Gaius Suetonius Tranquillus, who particularly enjoyed scandals.) Today there is some tendency to vindicate Tiberius, pointing out that the machinery of state ran smoothly under his rule. Following the advice of Augustus, he did not strain its resources trying to extend the empire. Only those immediately around him had to fear his imperial paranoia or sense of persecution.

It was under Tiberius that the danger of dictatorship became increasingly clear. The emperor did not delegate responsibility to his advisors and lacked the ability to administer the government alone. Few were brave enough to give him honest advice. (When Tiberius made his first appearance in the Senate as princeps, a senator was foolish enough to say, "Tell us, Caesar, which portion of power do you want to reserve for yourself?" When Tiberius reacted with an irritated gesture, the shocked senator hurriedly added, "I say this because we cannot go on without the unity of leadership and power in your hands.")

The misanthropic emperor evidently trusted only one man in the empire, Sejanus, leader of the praetorian cohorts. This corps of elite soldiers served as imperial bodyguard, stationed around the palace in Rome and in certain strategic locations on the Italian peninsula. Only the most trusted confidant of any emperor could be appointed as commander of the guard.

It was obvious to everyone that Sejanus wanted to use this trust to be designated as imperial successor. He entangled the emperor's relatives in a mesh of intrigues, acquiring such influence over Tiberius that the leader himself opened the way for him. One by one, Tiberius eliminated his relatives on charges of treason. Sejanus's influence continued to grow. In AD 26, the aging emperor yielded to it, retreating to the island of Capri. He left imperial control

for the moment in the hands of the prefect of Rome.

Sejanus remained near Rome with most of the guard. He functioned as caretaker and protector to Tiberius, determining the news he received. The Senate could only watch as the commander of the guard misused the power Tiberius increasingly delegated to him. There was no doubt now that Sejanus had been chosen as successor. A number of influential senators protested to Tiberius, letting it be known that they would oppose him if Sejanus did not disappear from the scene. The commander panicked, making hasty plans for a coup, perhaps exactly what his opponents wanted. Tiberius, advised of the plot, acted immediately to arrest Sejanus and his supporters. All were put to death for treason in AD 31.

Senators who thought that the elimina-

Mass of rock on the island of Capri, to which the Emperor Tiberius retired in AD 26. From there, he ruled the empire through his trusted friend Sejanus, who unsuccesfully tried to overthrow the government.

AVGVSTO XIII   M·PLAVTIOSILVAN   COS·

V·S·DEIASODIVCILIVS·DESALVIVS·BRINNIVS·PRINCEPS·L·FVR·INSEESAIVIVS
MAG·   VICI·   SANDALIARS·

Roman marble altar for the house gods, the *lares*, on which the deified Emperor August is depicted as a soothsayer: he is carrying the ritual scepter in his right hand.

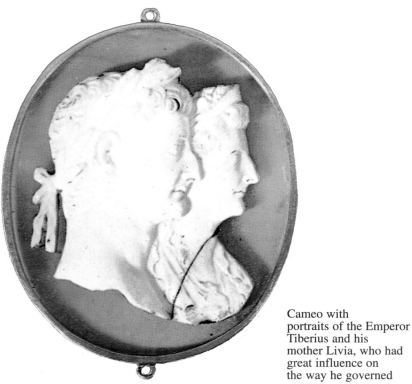

Cameo with portraits of the Emperor Tiberius and his mother Livia, who had great influence on the way he governed

tion of Sejanus would lead to a moderation of imperial policy were disappointed. Gossip and paranoia were the hallmarks of his reign. Betrayal by his closest confidant only deepened Tiberius's sense of mistrust. He began to show definite signs of mental illness, suspicious of everyone. He did not return to Rome, continuing to rule by letter from Capri. Meanwhile, in the capital, rumors began to circulate about orgies he was said to be having in the gigantic caves on the island. (While these have kept popular imagination busy for centuries, there is no solid evidence to substaniate them.) Other rumors (also unsubstantiated) said that he had arranged for the murder of his own heir apparent and nephew,

Germanicus. This man had both great personal charm and a number of campaigns to his name in Germany. Tiberius hated and distrusted him. When Germanicus died in the east after a short illness, Tiberius's viceroy, Piso, was generally suspected of poisoning him.

Tiberius's rule from Capri created great uncertainty and pressure in Rome. Those discredited by Sejanus found the emperor's trust in them still not restored. New plots abounded, but Tiberius received plenty of information from *delatores* (informers who acted as public prosecutors). A system of "state prosecution" as we understand it today did not exist; instead it was left to private citizens to make accusations. Akin to our concept of treason, the Romans referred to the *lex maiestatis* as anything that might defame the "majesty" of Rome and her people. Informers of high treason were *delatores maiestatis*. An entire profession of *delatores* arose in Rome, informers who checked up on people's actions and told the princeps on the least suspicion. Once they accused someone, that individual had little chance to clear his name. His friends would not dare help. In fact, the opposite was true: they would applaud the condemnation to save their own lives. It did not take much for the emperor to have one executed. There was a sigh of relief when Rome learned of Tiberius's death in AD 37. He was not deified as Caesar and Augustus had been before him.

Caligula (Emperor: AD 37–41)
Tiberius had two adult heirs, his great-nephew, whom he had adopted as a son,

Roman arch at Orange, in the French Provence. This arch was rebuilt by Tiberius on the ruins of an earlier one from Caesar's reign. The reliefs depict Roman soldiers in battle.

and his grandson. Upon his death, the Senate immediately recognized the first, Gaius, as his successor, although little was known about him. It was reported that his soldiers adored him and that his father Germanicus had dressed him in miniature uniforms as a child. This had given him his nickname Caligula (or Little Boots).

At first it looked as if Caligula would rule with the personal manner of his popular father. The first months of his reign were like a breath of fresh air. The delatores fell victim to persecution, pol-

The start of a banquet at the house of a well-to-do Roman family, as shown on a fresco from Pompeii. Servants wash the hands and feet of the guests.

itical prisoners were given amnesty, and the new princeps distinguished himself by great generosity. That all changed quickly. Historically regarded as mad, Caligula had a despotic character. Incapable of playing the mild benefactor, he strove for absolute power of the kind the Hellenistic kings had possessed, unhampered by any tradition or elite. Caligula had himself deified during his lifetime and seemed to take himself as a god quite seriously. Deification, normally posthumous, usually meant little more than ceremony, a senatorial token of respect.

Caligula, however, had personal altars to himself erected all over the empire. He had a bridge built between his palace on the Palatine Hill in Rome and the temples on

the Capitoline so he could communicate easily with Jupiter.

This divine mania brought Caligula into serious conflict with the Jews. They refused to worship any other God than their own Yahweh (Jehovah). Neither Augustus nor Tiberius had seen reason to persecute them for this, but their obstinacy infuriated Caligula. He ordered an image of himself to be erected in the inner sanctum of the Jewish temple. He organized a mob in Alexandria and gave it official permission to hunt down Jews. The victims were compelled to worship a statue of him. The Jews hoped for restitution from the unbalanced princeps. Imperial administration outside Rome was generally benevolent and, in the provinces, the emperors were considered competent and fair. Corruption or tyranny were usually blamed on bad officials below their notice.

A mission was sent to Rome led by the famous philosopher Filo. The Alexandrian Jews were introduced to Caligula first as he was walking in his garden. The princeps agreed to listen to them the following day. When the Jews came back, however, they found he had left for Naples. A new meeting was arranged. Filo recounts:

The emperor had a favorite whom he could not leave alone for a minute. He played with him, he ate with him, he bathed with him. He joked with us to amuse him. He needed excuses to make his jokes and in the end he slandered us. When the emperor eventually received us, again in Rome, his behavior showed us that he would not be our judge, but our accuser. "Are you," he asked, "from that godless nation which has refused to make offerings to me and prefers to worship a god whose name you may not even speak?" And then the emperor raised his arms to heaven and uttered a curse which we cannot repeat.

According to Filo, the Jews excused themselves by saying that they had brought him offerings during his illness, in the hope that he would recover.

"That may be, but you made offers to another before me, and not to myself," Caligula interrupted them. In the meantime the emperor was talking to his attendants about a thousand different things, while he told them to decorate several rooms. Suddenly he spoke to the Jews and called, "Why don't you eat pork?"

Filo, who was the mission's spokesman, said, "That is our custom. There are others who don't eat lamb."

"And they are quite right," said Caligula. "The sheep has very bad flesh."

"Then," says Filo, "We decided to say

nothing more because we saw that he was enjoying throwing impolite sarcastic remarks at our heads."

Finally, the emperor asked irritably, "What is your law and your organization?"

The Jews took courage once more and began to explain, but the emperor had no patience and waved them away with the words, "I see that you are just a bunch of fools who deserve pity rather than punishment, since you don't believe I have a divine nature."

If Caligula thought Filo was stupid, one can imagine what Filo thought of Caligula.

Caligula, Roman emperor who ruled from AD 37 to 41

Marble relief showing a horse race. The charioteer is driving a four-horse chariot thundering toward a curve in the racecourse.

763

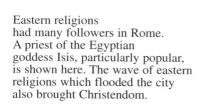

Anyone reading these texts would not be surprised to learn that frequent rebellions and mutinies occurred in the provinces. These were, in fact, expressions of local dissatisfaction which had little to do with Roman rule. Major rebellion in Judaea was only avoided by the local governor's decision to keep postponing Caligula's order that he be worshipped in the temple in Jerusalem.

The Romans, too, suffered under Caligula's reign of terror. On one occasion, displeased with the crowd in the stadium, the emperor had the games stopped, the sun shades removed, and the exits sealed off by soldiers. For the whole day, he enjoyed the sight of the thousands of spectators sitting in the burning sun without food or drink. Life was never a certainty in his presence. ("What a lovely neck!" he said once to one of his courtesans. "One word from me and it will fly off.")

Eventually, Caligula went north to muster an enormous army against Britannia. He had it assemble in battle array on the beaches of Normandy so that he could suddenly give the order...to gather shellfish. Nothing came of the expedition, although Caligula frequently boasted that he and his army had conquered the ocean.

Four years of such imperial behavior led to questions even among the praetorian guard. Its officers devised a plot and felled the mad princeps. The individual plotters regarded themselves as the heirs of Brutus and Cassius, who led the attack on Julius Caesar carried out on the Senate floor in 44 BC. Like the assassins of 44 BC, they were serious about restoring the Republic. Before they could attempt it, however, other praetorians took action.

Recognizing that their fate depended on who held the principate, these other praetorians considered it crucial to locate and install a new princeps as soon as possible. A few of the soldiers saw a pair of feet behind a curtain. They pulled the cloth away and found the terrified uncle of the murdered Caligula, Claudius. He apparently thought he was going to die, as well, but they took him to the inner courtyard and received him officially as the new emperor. Their swords constituted a powerful reminder to more tradition-minded republicans to hold their peace.

Portrait of Agrippina the Younger, Caligula's sister, who was married to the Emperor Claudius

Eastern religions had many followers in Rome. A priest of the Egyptian goddess Isis, particularly popular, is shown here. The wave of eastern religions which flooded the city also brought Christendom.

Claudius I (Emperor: AD 41–54)

A retiring man, ridiculed in the family for his stutter and his infirmities, Tiberius Claudius Drusus Nero Germanicus (born in 10 BC) had previously devoted himself to scholarship and the avoidance of public notice. Once in command, however, he proved effective, if controversial.

He reorganized the administration of the government bureaucracy, particularly with regard to financial affairs. As had been the imperial custom since Augustus, he managed the empire from his own household. A great deal went on in this particular house. Claudius had several wives who carried significant influence. He employed slaves and freedmen as secretaries. Appointed as the heads of the various departments on the basis of their own talents, they went on to acquire great power. Insolent and greedy, many abused their positions. The Roman aristocrats, many the victims of freedman ambition, resented it, recognizing that despite their lineage, they had nowhere near as much power as the freed slaves.

They hated men like Narcissus, who was in charge of correspondence, and Pallas, who dealt with finances.

Claudius himself showed great respect for the aristocracy and the Senate, according that body very much the role that Augustus had outlined. A strong advocate of the liberal granting of Roman citizenship in the provinces, he also put provincials directly into the Senate, assigning them whatever rank he chose. This relieved the favored ones of the inconvenience of ascending through the ranks. To avoid offending sitting senators, he raised many of them, in turn, to patrician status. Made censor in AD 47, the emperor could add senators at whim. (He also executed them at whim, for conspiracy or violation of state security.)

In the provinces, Claudius encouraged extensive Romanization policies. These tended to reduce the importance of the Italian peninsula in the Senate, a fact which did not add to his popularity there. On the peninsula itself, however, Claudius im-

Roman relief from the first century AD. A judge makes a sacrifice to the gods at the beginning of a military campaign.

765

The ruins of Ostia, the port of Rome. The Emperor Claudius had the harbor extended and deepened.

In the excavated city of Pompeii many millstones have been found. Donkeys, tied to a yoke, turned these millstones (which can also be seen in the illustration on page 824). This is how grain was finely ground and oil was pressed from olives.

proved government administration within the *municipiae* (municipal towns), had marshes drained, and had roads and harbors built. He was responsible for the harbor at Ostia, just south of Rome at the mouth of the Tiber and he restored several major aqueducts that brought water to Rome.

Overseas, Claudius expanded the empire, incorporating three client kingdoms (Mauretania in AD 42, Lycia in AD 43, and Thrace in AD 46). His greatest accomplishment in this regard was the annexation of Britannia. He personally led that conquest, begun in AD 43, to make up for his lack of military glory. It succeeded. Within the year, he returned in triumph to Rome and was given a victory procession.

Claudius was also noted for his intelligence. He was something of an amateur, self-taught architect, and he introduced three new characters to the Latin alphabet (although they later fell out of use). However, unlike many of the other emperors, Claudius did not build a forum and he did not add to the imperial palace on the Palatine.

Successful or not, Claudius was always widely detested. His wives were part of the

The Romans and Life after Death

To most of the people of ancient Rome, religion was not a source of hope for eternal life, but a vague idea of external power which they called *numina*. The Romans believed that carefully prescribed prayers and actions could affect numina favorably or unfavorably. They contended that the soul of the dead lived on, either in or around the grave.

Through contact first with Greek colonies in southern Italy and later with Greece itself, the Romans adopted classical Hellenistic mythology. Here they found a pantheon of gods, each one with a clearly defined task and personality, and a belief in life after death. The Greeks believed that the souls of the dead lived not in their graves but in the dark underworld.

However, the Romans continued to hold on to their own ideas about afterlife. They began to believe that besides the soul (or *anima*, a word which literally means breath or wind), something else remained after death, namely the *umbra* (or shadow). These shadows of the dead made up the large swarm of *manes* (a word always used in the plural). The manes could assist their families, appearing in dreams and revelations to advise, but could also turn against them. Those who offended the manes, trying to control them with magic potions, for example, would have evil spirits to deal with.

The shadows departed into the underworld through cracks in the earth. Charon, the ferryman, took them across the River of the Dead, the Styx, in a boat to be subjected to the judgment of two infallible judges.

Those condemned were thrown into the Tartarus for punishment. (One well-known story about such punishment concerns Tantalus, who was made to stand in water up to his lips with a branch of delicious fruit right in front of his face. When he wanted to take a drink, the water level would drop; when he wanted to pick some fruit, the branch would be blown away by the wind.

Those saved, however, were allowed to enter the Elysian Fields with their blossoming valleys and multicolored light. The poet Ovid claimed that the blessed replicated their earthly ways of life there.

Virgil told of the shadows of blessed ones who amused themselves by singing

and holding chariot races.

There were other philosophic ideas around which held that the soul is taken up between the stars after death. As the empire expanded, the Romans were further influenced by eastern cults like those of Isis, Mithras, and Christianity. Epitaphs, texts, and monuments reveal both skepticism about the the immortality of the soul and the great popularity of the new-found religions.

Relief from a Roman monumental tomb, representing the legend of Proserpina. Pluto, god of the underworld, had fallen in love with her; he abducted her to his realm.

problem. His wife Messalina even insulted him in public. The writers Tacitus and Suetonius tell wild stories about this woman. Young and beautiful, Messalina was said to be discontented with her deformed princeps and to have conspired to have him removed as emperor. She would call in young aristocrats from all over the city to spend the night with her, punishing any who refused with certain death. Eventually, she began an affair with the young Consul Gaius Silius. The final incident is reported to have occurred when the two conducted a wild party while Claudius (they thought) was away from the city. Claudius surprised his wife in the middle of the orgy, finding her dancing clothed only in a leopard skin. He had her locked away that night but by the next day seemed ready to grant her clemency, speaking of her as "that unfortunate." Before he could do so, the freed slave Narcissus arranged for her execution. Hardly regretful, Claudius married again shortly afterward.

Agrippina

His new wife was the devious and exquisitely lovely Agrippina. She was at once his own niece, the great-granddaughter of Caesar Augustus, and the ex-wife of the prominent Domitius Ahenobarbus. She brought with her a sixteen-year-old son from her first marriage, Lucius Domitius Ahenobarbus (born in AD 37), best known as Nero. It was Agrippina's sole ambition to make her son princeps and then to rule through him. Two people, however, stood in the way. Claudius himself and Britannicus, his son by Messalina (named obviously after Claudius's conquest of Britannia). Agrippina used her influence with Claudius to get him to adopt Nero in AD 50, thus making him equal to Britannicus. She had the emperor grant the young Nero extensive power outside Rome.

The empress then devoted herself to clearing Claudius himself out of the way, finally succeeding, it is said, by poisoning him with a plateful of mushrooms. Because of her influence over the influential praetorian guard, Agrippina had no trouble having Nero declared princeps. However, far too young to take control himself, the boy was placed under the regency of the wise old Stoic philosopher Seneca and the present commander of the praetorian guard, Burrus.

Statue of Emperor Claudius, who ruled from AD 41 to 54. One of the remarkable features of his rule was that he gave freed slaves an important role in running the empire.

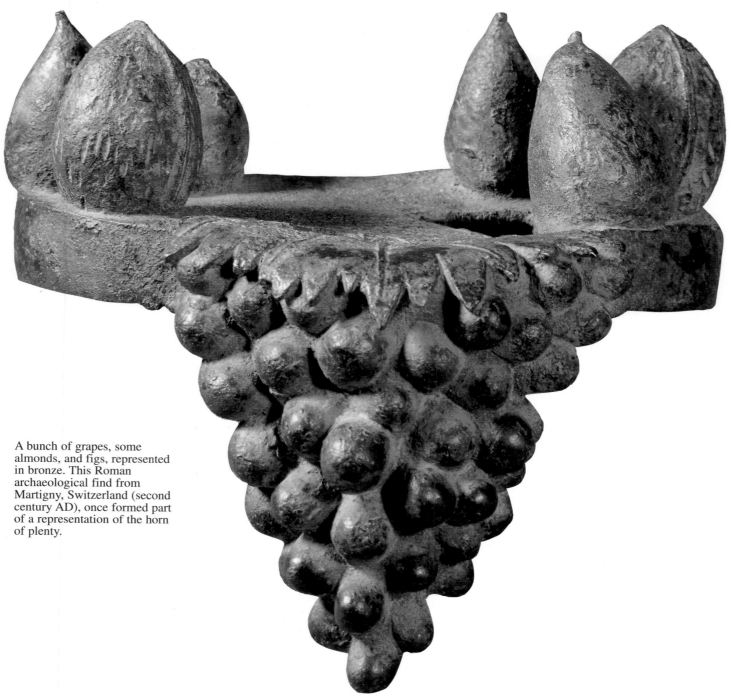

A bunch of grapes, some almonds, and figs, represented in bronze. This Roman archaeological find from Martigny, Switzerland (second century AD), once formed part of a representation of the horn of plenty.

Consolidation of Power

From Nero to the Flavian Emperors

Poisoned or not, Claudius was deified. The Temple of Divas Claudius was initiated after his death in AD 54. Nero, his despotic adopted son would not be. Quite the contrary: his reign would be removed from official Senate record.

The Julio-Claudian Emperors:
Nero (AD 54–68)
In AD 54, the situation appeared promising. Emperor at only seventeen years old, Nero initially was placed under the charge of his tutor Lucius Annaeus Seneca, the famous

Reconstruction model
of one of the bridges that
the Romans built
across the river Rhine

Stoic philosopher, and Sextus Affranius Burrus, Prefect of the Praetorian Guard. They had inherited a well-ordered empire from Claudius. Claudius had reorganized imperial finances. Taxes from all provinces were controlled centrally in Rome. State coffers were reasonably well filled. All over the empire, new colonies were being founded. Burrus and Seneca ruled in a strongly aristocratic manner, allowing little, if any, dissent but the empire prospered under them. The young Princeps Nero had no choice but to let them go their own way. In any case, he considered himself a great poet and singer and his ambitions, at first, lay mainly in the direction of such artistry. The situation was a great disappointment to the ambitious Agrippina. She wanted to take over from Seneca and Burrus and, without her son's support, she could not.

Within five years, Nero had evolved into a monster. He murdered, eventually, his stepbrother, his mother, his first and second wives, and his tutor.

Agrippina fought to keep her influence as many others tried to attach themselves to her son. According to Tacitus, Agrippina tried to seduce Nero during an orgy. Seneca, who witnessed this, sent in Acte, a beautiful freedwoman already involved with Nero. Agrippina's effort failed and, in reaction, she began to favor Britannicus, the son of Claudius and Nero's younger stepbrother. Nero had him poisoned.

By AD 59, now hating his interfering mother, Nero decided to get rid of her, as well. Burrus must have known about this and apparently did not object. The princeps invited his mother to one of his country houses, supposedly for a reconciliation. As the house was on a lake, he sent a ship to pick her up. The ship had been rigged to fall apart in the middle of the lake, but when that happened, Agrippina managed to swim to shore. The annoyed Nero gave up on subtlety and had a company of praeto-

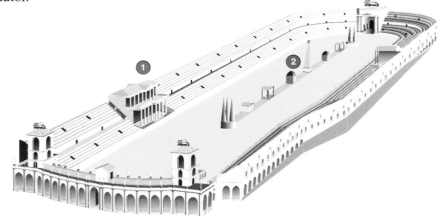

Reconstruction drawing of the Circus Maximus, at the foot of the Palatine Hill in Rome, after its extension in AD 64. Horse races were held in the circus, watched by the emperor and his following from a covered grandstand (1). In the center was the spina (2) with obelisks (stone pillars), columns, and fountains.

rians simply stab his mother to death. Burrus arranged for the Praetorian Guard to congratulate him openly on the death of Agrippina, circulating the rumor that she had conspired against Nero, despite the lack of evidence. Seneca wrote the text of a statement on this matter which the princeps read to the Senate.

The young emperor rapidly developed into a vicious and pleasure-seeking despot. His attitude was reinforced by his mistress Poppaea Sabina, the wife of Marcus Salvius Otho, and his villainous friend Tigellinus. Eventually, Nero divorced and then murdered his first wife Octavia, a daughter of Claudius. In AD 65, he kicked the unfortunate Poppaea to death, marrying Statilia Messalina after killing her husband.

After the unplanned death of Burrus, Seneca lost any remaining influence with the emperor. Nero's attention focused on Tigellinus, who replaced Burrus as head of the Praetorian Guard. His flattery convinced Nero that he was indeed a talented singer and poet. The emperor even went so far as to appear on stage in public. Naturally, the audience was obliged to applaud enthusiastically.

It is impossible to assess whether or not Nero actually had any talent. According to the senators and historians of the time, such as Tacitus, the emperor made a fool of himself. His performances, it was said, brought disgrace upon his family and the whole of the Roman aristocracy. Nero even traveled to Greece to exhibit his talent. Of course, wherever he went, he won prizes. At the Olympic Games in AD 66, he took part in the chariot races, but his chariot was so wide that no other competitors could get on the track with him. The princeps, as the only participant, was awarded the crown of laurel leaves.

In AD 64, most of Rome burned to the ground. It is not clear how this particular one started, but fires broke out regularly in the huge city with its maze of narrow streets, crowded with wooden facades and balconies. A wall of fire and smoke swept through the alleyways for days on end, destroying the flimsy houses of Rome's poor. Thousands died. Afterward, rumor had it that Nero had stood on a hill watching the flames, singing a song he had written about the fall of Troy. Many people wondered if Nero himself had started the fire. Such rumors annoyed him. He decided to find a way to divert popular attention away from himself.

Christians in Rome

For several years, a new sect had been operating in and around Rome. Originating in Palestine, its members worshipped the god of the Jews, rather than the multiplicity of Roman deities. They met on a fixed day each week. People called them Christians, after the founder of the sect, called Jesus Christ, who had been crucified under

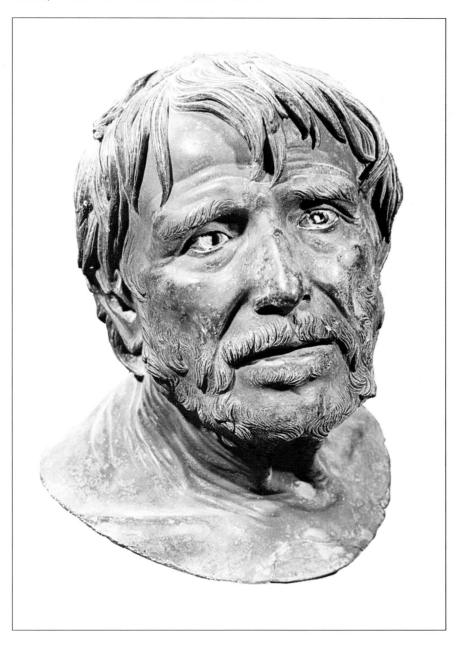

Tiberius. (Death by crucifixion, nailing the victim to a wooden cross by his hands and feet, was the usual criminal punishment among the Romans at the time.) It was said that the Christians expected this Christ to return to Earth soon and to punish the whole of what they claimed to be the sinful world.

The average Roman paid little attention. There were many eastern sects in Rome and many with unfortunate reputations. People suspected, for instance, that the

Portrait of Lucius Annaeus Seneca, the famous philosopher who was also advisor to the courts of Caligula and Claudius, and instructor to the later Emperor Nero

Christians carried out all sorts of crimes during their meetings.

Nero thought the situation perfect for exploitation. The persecution he began claimed hundreds of victims. Many victims were martyred in the Circus of Nero, adjacent to what is now St. Peter's Church, whose obelisk now stands directly in front of the facade of the church. Some Christians, when arrested, gave the names of other believers. This led to the full-scale persecution of multitudes of Christians, not so much for starting the fire as for their ideas about the end of the world. Construed to be a threat to Rome (although they were talking about an inner kingdom, not a temporal one), Christians were executed gruesomely during the games in the amphitheater. Some were covered in pitch and used as live human torches during the emperor's parties.

Tacitus notes that such cruelty eventually made people sympathetic to the Christians, although most still felt that their barbarous beliefs deserved the death penalty. In any case, the rumor that Nero had started the fire himself refused to die down, despite the fate of the Christians. Their persecution did not put an end to the Christian sect in Rome.

It is important to note that many Christians were Roman citizens and therefore permitted the protection of Roman law. When, after having been flogged, Paul the Apostle said, "Civis Romanus sum" ("I am a Roman citizen"); the city council came to

Bust of the Emperor Nero, who ruled from AD 54 to 68

Bust of Gaius Domitius Corbulo, who served as general in the armies of the Emperors Claudius and Nero. Corbulo achieved victories over the Germans and Parthians.

apologize. It was not permitted to flog a Roman. The apostle could have made trouble at the highest level. Noncitizens were subject to arbitrary martial law. The governor could condemn them to death without a second thought, as Pontius Pilate did with Jesus. Paul, however, appealed to the emperor and was brought to Rome. There he died by the sword, the legally prescribed manner of execution, while the Jew Peter, who did not have Roman citizenship, was crucified upside down, at his own request. He did not wish to preempt the symbol that the crucifixion of Christ had already become.

Despite the fact that these major leaders, Peter and Paul, were killed, the sect was not destroyed. Various sources indicated that Christianity, in fact, remained one of the more successful sects in Rome. It would eventually prove to be the most successful.

Rebuilding Rome

While Rome was being rebuilt, Nero decided to make it more magnificent than ever. With his staff, he drew up an impressive plan for a *rus in urbe* (a villa in the city). (A lake in the gardens surrounding his palace would much later be covered by the Roman Colosseum.) The city would be reconstructed in a much more logical manner than before. Strict building regulations prescribed solid construction and the use of fireproof materials for all new buildings. The streets would be made wider.

Nero was primarily interested in his palace, the *Domus Aurea* (Golden House). The Golden House was decorated with frescoes whose "grotesque" motifs deeply influenced Renaissance artists, e.g., Raphael, whose decorations in the Vatican palace reflect what he saw of the ruined Domus Aurea in the early 16th century.

Even today, anyone seeing the ruins of its arched roofs is impressed by its overwhelming size. Yet it was never finished, owing to Nero's chronic shortage of money. A major reason for his getting involved in government was to raise more money through taxes, particularly from the provinces, a fact which led to widespread discontent.

Rebellion against Nero

Provincial inhabitants resented the venality and cruelty of Nero's administrators, especially in Britain. In AD 60, smoldering rage flared into open rebellion there, led by Queen Boudicca. Thousands of natives were killed and the settlements of Camulodunum (Colchester), Verulamium (St. Al-

bans), and Londinium (the eventual London) were razed before the Romans regained control the next year.

From AD 62 to 65, the prestigious Roman General Corbulo directed a military campaign to establish Armenia as a buffer state against Parthia. He would die by suicide at the end of that year, proven one of the conspirators in a plot to replace Nero.

In Rome itself, Nero's administrative misconduct and the growing insecurity he provoked among the senators fostered popular discontent and attitudes of rebellion. The notable Gaius Calpurnius Piso and 41 prominent Romans initiated a conspiracy to unseat him. Nero discovered it in AD 65 and ordered Piso and his fellow conspira-tors to death. Among them was Seneca, the former tutor and government minister. Realizing that taking their own lives was preferable to waiting for Nero's executioners, 18 of them slit their own wrists in a hot bath.

Jewish Revolt

Roman brutality, fed by Jewish rage, fomented Jewish revolution in Judaea in AD 66. Jewish resistance increased in the provinces, as well. Julius Alexander, Prefect of Egypt, moved to repress any involvement by the Jews there. Disorder spread throughout the country.

Emperor Nero sent in Titus Flavius Vespasianus (Vespasian) to end the revolt. Completing a bloody campaign against the

One of the walls, colorfully decorated with frescoes, of the *Domus Aurea* (Golden House) which Nero had built in a part of Rome that had been destroyed by fire.

A row of standards (*insignia*) belonging to three Roman legions and the Praetorian Guard (*on the right*).

cide. The victorious general said he was acting for the Senate, not for Nero. Galba advanced on Rome without opposition, having bribed the praetorians to support the revolt.

Nero's Death

It was June 9, AD 68. Without the allegiance of even the Praetorian Guard and declared an outlaw by the Senate, Nero fled the city. Soldiers sent to arrest the tyrant were too late. "What a great artist dies with me!" he is said to have murmured as, with the help of a faithful slave, the princeps stabbed himself in the throat with a dagger. He was 31 years old.

The sources available to us on that time are written primarily from the viewpoint of senators of the old Republic. What they considered tyranny might well have been seen by the common man in Rome, at least, as a wonderful means of civic control. While it is known that Nero was unpopular in the provinces, which he exploited to the benefit of Rome, it is difficult to judge how the average Roman felt about his princeps. There is reason to believe his opinions might have been quite different from those in the Senate.

The tyranny of the princeps had rarely affected the people in the alleyways of Rome. They had probably only noticed, with relish, that powerful and corrupt men were getting massacred by the hundreds. Furthermore, Nero had spent vast sums, more than any other princeps, on *panem et circenses* (bread and circuses).

The poet Juvenal, writing several decades after Nero's death, may have been right when he said that was all the masses wanted. In any case, when the fact of Nero's death became known, all Rome mourned. Shopkeepers closed their shops. For years afterward, fresh flowers were placed on the simple burial mound the freedwoman Acte erected for her imperial lover.

Whatever the popular assessment of Nero, the official end to the Julio-Claudian dynasty that died with him was hardly glorious. Declared *damnatio memoriae* (damned in memory) by the Senate, Nero's imperial reign was obliterated from the official record. Later, under Domitian, even building inscriptions were erased.

Brief Reigns:
Galba, Otho, and Vitellius (AD 68–69)

The Senate recognized the victorious Galba as princeps. The new emperor was not connected to the house of Augustus in any way. The last barrier to the principate had been removed. If Galba could become

Jews, village by village, he began a siege of Jerusalem. In the city, conditions became intolerable. Before the situation could be resolved, two provincial governors rebelled in the west.

The first was Julius Vindex, governor of Gallia Lugdunensis, soon joined by Sulpicius Galba, governor of Hispania Tarraconensis. In AD 68, Roman legions on the Rhine slaughtered the native Gauls in Vindex's army, forcing their leader to sui-

princeps (and at age 73 he did) so could any of the aristocracy. Rome was to have a difficult year under three emperors in rapid succession. (A fourth, taking over at the end of AD 69, would last longer.)

For the first time in a hundred years, fighting was rampant in the streets. Battles, murder, and pillage were commonplace. The new Princeps Galba, making efforts to hoard a treasury squandered by Nero, was popular with no one. His legions fought each other. Those in the north, who had engineered Nero's downfall, barely knew him. They felt they had been used to put a stranger in power. Shortly after he was recognized as princeps, Galba learned that the northern legions under Aulus Vitellius, Legate of Germania Inferior (Lower Germany), were in revolt, preparing to bring their candidate to Rome. Galba adopted an accomplished military man and assigned him the task of fighting the rebellion on his behalf.

This offended Marcus Salvius Otho, a prominent banker and Poppaea Sabina's first husband, who had hoped to succeed Galba. Otho bought off the Praetorian Guards. Galba was murdered in the street by his own bodyguard. Otho was made emperor of a state in turmoil. Meanwhile, Vitellius and his troops advanced southward. Otho led the Praetorian Guard and a hastily formed army to face him. Defeated near Cremona in northern Italy, he committed suicide.

In April, AD 69, Vitellius and his Rhineland army entered Rome. Recognized by the Senate as princeps, Vitellius was

Cameo with the portrait of the Emperor Galba, who succeeded Nero

Roman relief: insignia belonging to various legions can be distinguished in the background.

775

defeated, in turn, in a battle at Bedriacum by Titus Flavius Vespasian.

The Flavian Emperors: Vespasian (AD 69–79)

It was not only the legions on the Rhine border who wanted one of their own as princeps. Those in Judaea had the same idea. Vespasian commanded the huge army that had assembled since AD 66 around Jerusalem to suppress the great Jewish rebellion. Its soldiers nominated him as princeps. He quickly gained support throughout the region and even from the

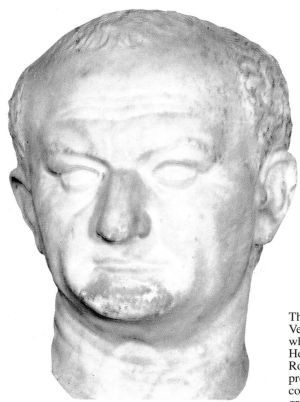

The Emperor Titus Flavius Vespasianus (Vespasian), who ruled from AD 69 to 79. He stimulated the Romanization of the provinces by founding colonies and by granting Roman citizenship to their inhabitants.

legions along the Danube. After the defeat and death of Vitellius, the acquiescent Senate gave him the title the legions wanted him to have. It was December 22, AD 69.

The Senate acted through the *Lex de Imperio Vespasiani* (the law conferring imperial power on Vespasian), the first time it had passed such a law. Fragments of the actual parchment are preserved today in Rome.

Vespasian was not a descendant of the old Roman aristocracy. Born in a small Italian town, he did not even come from Rome. His family had only recently been promoted to the senatorial order. Yet the outsider emperor took over the empire with a firm hand.

A Rebellion in the North

In Germania Inferior (Lower Germany), the boggy Rhine delta where Gallic and German peoples lived under Roman military command, Batavians, called barbarians by the Romans, retained their own identity. Not only were they not made slaves to the Romans, they had formed an alliance whereby they delivered auxiliary troops led by their own officers. Called *foederati* (allies), they were on good terms with the Romans.

When the Romans started to interfere in the organization of these auxiliaries during the last years of Nero's government, the Batavians were deeply offended. In the chaos of AD 69, they mounted a rebellion under the leadership of Julius Civilis, a German who had obtained Roman citizenship after making a career in the army. Joined by Gallic troops, they took over most of the Roman camps along the Rhine. Vespasian ordered in Petilius Cerealis, who was able to negotiate an end to the rebellion by AD 70.

Relief showing a Roman soldier encamped in Alta Germania, in the region of what is modern Wiesbaden, Germany

The ruins of the Amphitheatrum Flavium, the Colosseum, built by order of the Emperor Vespasian in Rome. It was here that contests took place between heavily armed gladiators, who also often had to fight wild animals.

Vespasian's rule was authoritarian. He mercilessly eliminated all opposition, including annoying philosophers, banishing them from the capital. He took over as censor and stuffed the Senate with his supporters. Allowing it very little power, he did draw from it for administrative personnel. A nonaristocrat himself, Vespasian greatly increased the number of senators from the provinces. Under his reign, a new aristocracy based on government service gained ground.

Nero had left behind financial and organizational chaos. Vespasian solved the financial problems by cutting down drastically on spending and increasing taxes, including a poll tax on Jews. While he took great care not to antagonize the soldiers, many citizens felt victimized by his policies.

Vespasian even taxed the contents of the public urinals, which leatherworkers used to tan their hides. A delegation went to the emperor to ask him to lift the tax. Vespasian held a coin in front of their noses and asked, "Does this stink?" Despite his spending cutbacks, Vespasian wanted to invest in something useful. He halted construction on Nero's Golden House and had the huge Flavian amphitheater built on the site for the people. (In the Middle Ages, the Romans renamed this the Colosseum, after the colossus, a huge statue of Nero nearby.)

Serious problems were underway in the north. Sarmatian people raided on the Danube. Vespasian's generals restored law and order there relatively quickly. In Germania Inferior (Lower Germany), it was another question. Fiercely independent Batavian people, a source of auxiliary troops for Rome, resented the increasingly authoritarian way they were being treated and rebelled. It took a year to negotiate a settlement in AD 70.

That same year, Titus, the elder son of Vespasian, took Jerusalem for his father, finally ending the long war in Judaea. The year had made one thing clear: the power of a princeps rested on the support of his army.

Vespasian's harsh rule lasted ten years. He groomed his sons throughout to succeed him. When he sensed that his end was near, he said, "Oh dear, I think I'm turning into a god." Indeed, his son Titus, succeeding him without problem, promptly had him deified.

The Flavian Emperors: Titus (AD 79–81)

Titus lived only two years after inheriting the imperial mantle. His major accomplishment had occurred before he was emperor: the conquering of Jerusalem in AD 70. He had destroyed the temple (except for a piece still called the Wailing Wall) and slaughtered most of the people.

In AD 79, during his short and otherwise unremarkable reign, the volcano Mount Vesuvius, near Naples, erupted, covering the nearby towns of Pompeii and Herculaneum with 13 feet (four meters) of hot ash and burying the people alive.

The city of Pompeii had been ravaged by an earthquake some years earlier (in AD 63). At that time, Vesuvius had contributed to the disaster with poisonous gas and smothering tons of volcanic ash and mud. This time, the volcano totally obliterated the city.

Pompeii would remain buried for 1500 years; excavation began in the eighteenth century. It was discovered that the ash, leached by hundreds of years of rain, had formed perfect molds around the bodies of the long dead townspeople. Archaeologists were able to pour plaster into these molds and create perfect replicas, horrifying but amazingly informative. The ancient city forms a sculpture of its own past.

The short-lived Titus had a subsequent and relatively smaller catastrophe to contend with in his two-year reign: yet

Aerial photograph of the Piazza Navona in Rome, which clearly shows the form of the old Roman circus that was used for chariot races

Ruins of an ancient Roman city near Caunus, Turkey. Some Byzantine remains have been found here also.

another major fire in Rome. His efforts to help its survivors and the overall kindness and justice with which he governed resulted in his subsequent posthumous deification. He was succeeded by his brother Domitian, whose name would become synonymous with terror.

The Emperor Titus, Vespasian's oldest son and successor

The Triumphal Arch of Titus at the Forum Romanum, erected by the Senate in memory of the siege and conquest of Jerusalem

Romanization of the Empire

Domitian and the Antonine Emperors

The Flavian Emperors: Domitian (AD 81–96)

The younger brother of Titus, second son of Vespasian, had never been designated as heir apparent, but after the death of Titus, he was first hailed as the new princeps by the Praetorian Guard and then approved by the Senate. A ruthless and suspicious man,

never before able to reach a position of influence because both his father and his brother had considered his sense of ambition dangerous, he suddenly had full power in his hands. He used it to instigate a reign of terror.

Contemptuous of the Senate, he manipulated it to a greater extent than any emperor

After the victory of the Emperor Trajan over the Dacians (a people that lived in the country now called Romania), a memorial column was erected. Its reliefs tell the story of the Dacian campaign. This detail shows a number of the peole the Romans called "barbarians."

Nerva, who was proclaimed emperor in AD 96 by the assassins of Domitian, the emperor who had ruled Rome as a brutal tyrant

before him. Yet he also insisted that the Senate accord him the complete respect he felt he merited, meting out severe punishment for any insult, real or imagined. He maintained control over Senate membership through both selection and, later, execution. He assured that senator-picking control by his status as *census perpetuus* (perpetual censor) beginning in AD 85. Repeatedly managing to get himself elected consul, the civilian head of government, he also continued to keep the allegiance of his troops.

He sent competent, incorruptible men (usually choosing his imperial civil service from the Senate or the equites) to the provinces, which thrived under his reign at first. He refined and enlarged the machinery of the state. Convinced that his position depended on the good will of the masses, he entertained them with spectacu-

lar events. These included two triumphal processions through Rome to honor his army's success against tribes in the northeast and the staging of large-scale games in the amphitheaters.

From the beginning, the princeps insisted that he was divine, requiring people to address him as *dominus et deus* (lord and god). During the first few years of his reign, he apparently did not need to demonstrate the godlike absolute control over human life he was to exhibit later. That changed in AD 89, when Saturninus, Roman commander on the Rhine, had himself declared princeps and began a rebellion. The emperor ended the revolt in a bloodbath of executions. Now he would trust no one. He kept the *delatores* (the informers) busy looking for conspiracy. In the senatorial order, nobody's life was safe. He simply executed anyone voicing opposition to him. Domitian himself became mad with fear of personal attack. He put up mirrors in every room so he could always see who was behind him.

His fears eventually led to his mismanagement of the empire. After fifteen years, his mirrors could not protect him. In AD 96, he was, indeed, the victim of the conspiracy he always feared. Even his own wife took part. A slave was hired to assassinate him. Like Nero, he was declared damnatio memoriae (damned in memory) and stricken from official record by the Senate. It ordered his name removed from all public buildings.

Domitian's military accomplishments, however, were not dismantled. Under the Flavian dynasty, as part of the effort in AD 69 to reduce the chance of their organization, native auxiliary forces were sent to serve far from their points of origin and generally placed under the command of officers of different ethnic makeup. They were assigned functions increasingly similar to those once performed by the regular legionnaires, working in small highly active detachments. (Traditional legions themselves, based in stone encampments, had grown less and less mobile.) Domitian continued these policies, using them to good effect in Britain, along the Rhine and the Danube, and on the eastern frontier.

Britain expanded between AD 71 and 84, under Flavian governors Petilius Cerealis (who had put down the Rhineland rebellion in AD 70), Julius Frontinus, and Julius Agricola. Under Domitian, the province included Wales, northern England, and parts of Scotland.

In AD 74, Vespasian took over a triangle of land between the Rhine and the Danube Rivers. Domitian followed, building extensive fortifications along the border. He turned the military regions of Upper and Lower Germany into regular provinces.

In AD 85 and 86, the powerful Dacian King Decebalus had crossed the Danube, invading from the north. Domitian stopped him in AD 88 but had to divert Roman resources to put down Saturninus in AD 89 and could not continue fighting the Dacian's later incursions. By the time Domitian died, the result was a negotiated frontier: Domitian paid Decebalus an annual sum to protect the lower Danube from Sarmatian attack.

In the east, Domitian, last of the Flavians, completed the development of military roads undertaken in Asia Minor by Vespasian, kept Judaea under control by sending in permanent legions, and rein-

Trajan the Spaniard was Nerva's adopted son and successor. He was the first non-Italian to be Roman Emperor.

Roman Empire, 272 BC
Expansion, 272–201 BC
Expansion, 201–133 BC
Expansion, 133–44 BC
Expansion, 44 BC–AD 117

ATLANTIC OCEAN
Hadrian's Wall
BRITAIN
BARBARIAN PEOPLES
GAUL (FRANCE)
The River Rhine
The River Rhône
IBERIA (SPAIN)
Corsica
Rome
ITALY
Sardinia
The River Danube
BLACK SEA
MACEDONIA
ASIA MINOR
MEDITERRANEAN SEA
Sicily
GREECE
Crete
Cyprus
NORTH-AFRICA
EGYPT
N
0   500 Km

The expansions of the Roman Empire up to the Golden Age under the Emperor Trajan (AD 98–117)

forced a Roman military presence by establishing legionary camps at major crossing points along the Euphrates.

The Antonine Emperors:
Nerva (AD 96–98)

The assassins of Domitian in the Senate quickly nominated one of their own as princeps, the elderly Senator Marcus Cocceius Nerva. He would be the first in a sequence of five superb rulers, called the Antonine emperors after their finest representative, Antoninus Pius. Interested in using his power wherever possible to put right the damage caused by his predecessor, Nerva introduced a law to provide relief for

Triumphal arch erected at Beneventum in honor of the Emperor Trajan. The reliefs on the left and right represent his life.

poor children in Italy. His focus on social problems made him beloved by citizens and senators but not by the still-loyal soldiers of Domitian. Lacking any military prestige, Nerva adopted a soldier as heir apparent, ignoring potential candidates among his own family. His choice was excellent: the Spanish officer Marcus Ul-

pius Trajanus (called Trajan), commander of the troops in Upper Germany.

Nerva died three months later and was treated to the deification customarily accorded fair and reasonable emperors. This initiated a tradition of adopting a successor on the basis of ability rather than family ties. The new custom would provide Rome with what history has termed the "good emperors" for the next century, a period when the principate flourished.

The Antonine Emperors:
Trajan the Conqueror (AD 98–117)

The Senate was obliged to accept Trajan as princeps, since he was the son of Nerva. He was the first emperor to be adopted unrelated by birth or marriage to any imperial line before him.

Trajan was in Germany when Nerva died. Still needed in the north, he did not bother to return to Rome until the following year. This indicated, at once, the high opinion he held of his immediate task, his commitment to the provinces, and the fact that he was not impressed by republican tradition. He apparently considered his nomination by the Senate nothing more than a formality. A provincial Spaniard himself, he would do well with the increasingly provincial Senate. Yet because he did not seek multiple offices simultaneously or the self-aggrandizement of many honored titles, he managed to endear himself to the more aristocratic side of the Senate at the same time

Unthreatening, if powerful, he allayed the fears of terror and conspiracy of the Domitian era. On the other hand, he did not hesitate to intervene in the Senate as he felt necessary. The new emperor was known in Rome as an outstanding ruler with high moral values. Once, when handing over a sword to the commander of the Praetorian Guard, he is reported to have said, "Use it against me if I neglect my duty, but use it to defend me if I perform my duty well."

Trajan ruled with a group of advisors about whom little is known. His domestic efforts revolved around pleasing the populace. He provided gladiatorial games for popular entertainment. He sponsored new buildings in Rome and public works in Italy: the construction and maintenance of buildings, harbors (he enlarged Claudius's port at Ostia), and roads (his Via Traiana replaced the Via Appia as the main highway between Beneventum and the port of Brundisium). Trajan sent *curatores* (financial experts) throughout the empire offering monetary advice. They also made low-cost loans available to farmers and used

Rebellion in the East

To the Romans, the Jews were a strange people. They worshipped only one god, for whom they were not allowed to make any statues, and they had serious disagreements among themselves about the interpretation of their holy scriptures. Moreover, they fanatically refused to worship the Roman emperor, their oppressor, as a god.

The Jews were, in fact, divided into two groups. The Sadducees, from the Roman point of view, were an enlightened people, more or less Hellenistic, from the higher classes who did not take their religion too seriously. They were on relatively good terms with the Romans. The other group were the Pharisees, who practiced an orthodox Judaism and remained firmly opposed to Roman influence and rule. They were not, however, interested in violent actions, unlike the Zealots who had taken up arms and carried on a sort of guerrilla warfare. Jewish resistance increased.

By AD 66, the inhabitants of Jerusalem drove the soldiers of the Roman garrison out of the city. Disorder spread throughout the country. Emperor Nero called on Vespasian to end the revolt. Completing a bloody campaign against the Jews, village by village, he began a siege of Jerusalem, unable to attack because of the political developments in that year.

When Vespasian's son Titus took over his father's command in AD 70, he quickly conquered Jerusalem, destroying the temple (except for a piece still called the Wailing Wall) and slaughtering most of the people.

The survivors were dealt with severely. Not allowed to rebuild their own temple, they had to pay for the building of one for the Roman god Jupiter Capitolinus. The Jews would rebel again seventy years later, only to be beaten once again after two years. The survivors would be scattered throughout the empire (in what is called the Diaspora).

Relief of the triumphal arch of the Emperor Titus, depicting the entry into Rome of the Roman soldiers who had crushed the rebellion in Judaea. As a victory symbol, they carry the most important trophy: the seven-branched candlestick (menorah) they took away after destroying the temple at Jerusalem.

The Romans liked to use natural barriers to protect their empire against invasions from barbarian tribes. On this fragment of Trajan's Column, three Roman soldiers can be seen guarding a frontier post on a riverbank

Ruins of the thermae (public baths) built in Rome under Trajan

the interest earned for children's charity.

Through the curatores, Trajan took over the senatorial provinces of Bithynia and Achaea, both on the verge of bankruptcy. His surviving correspondence with Pliny the Younger, whom he appointed as advisor to Bithynia, offers an in-depth look at the emperor's considerable administrative ability and attention to detail.

Trajan was first and foremost a soldier. He spent seven of his nineteen years in power in army camps and he died in an army tent. He deliberately broke with the precepts set by Augustus which advised consolidation of empire rather than additional conquest.

His greatest military achievement would be on the Danube. The Dacians had established a powerful empire in the Carpathian region under their King Decebalus. Domitian, in prior conflict with the Dacians, had been forced to sign a peace treaty paying them subsidies in return for their police efforts against the invasion-prone Sarmatian tribes on the Danube. Trajan resented this. Conflict flared in AD 102–103. The princeps personally led a campaign to subjugate Dacia. He built a massive stone bridge over the Danube to provide ready access across it. Decebalus and the Dacians, festering under Roman conquest, tried battle yet again (AD 105–106). This time, unable to stop Trajan's legions from entering their capital, the desperate Decebalus committed suicide. All Dacians refusing to surrender were hunted down and killed. The war destroyed Dacian identity. Although it was one of the cruelest campaigns in the history of Rome, Trajan erected a huge stone column to commemorate it in the fine new forum he had just completed. The reliefs on the column represented images of the campaign. (Trajan's Column, financed by spoils from the Dacian campaign, is still in existence.) A Latin dialect, influenced by the conquerors, would develop in the new province, attesting to the complete obliteration of Dacia. The language became Rumanian.

Trajan continued his conquests, annexing the kingdom of Arabia Petraea in AD 106, adding the buffer state of Armenia to the empire and invading Parthia in AD 114.

By AD 116, he had conquered (but not consolidated) Mesopotamia, sailing down the Tigris with his armies to the Persian Gulf. Fighting spread in his wake as Jews, Parthians, and other conquered peoples rose in revolution.

Trajan died in his tent in Syria in AD 117 without designating an heir. His widow claimed he had adopted Publius Aelius Hadrianus, his closest male relative and governor of Syria, on his deathbed. The emperor was routinely deified.

Hadrian the Administrator (AD 117–138)
Primarily on the strength of his widow's statement, Trajan's soldiers nominated Hadrian, another nonaristocratic Spaniard, as successor. Hadrian informed the Senate of this but did not bother to have his nomination endorsed, so weak was senatorial power.

A civilian rather than a soldier, Hadrian renounced his predecessor's aggressive policies, foregoing new conquests in Asia. Hadrian is best known as an excellent administrator. He implemented a policy of frontier protection rather than expansion, which made for a peaceful regime. Only in Judaea (now called Syria Palaestina) were there problems. He converted Jerusalem into a Roman colony, Aelia Capitolina, to the outraged and violent objection of Bar Kochba and his followers in AD 132–135.

The emperor set up strong fortifications, where necessary, to defend his borders. Hadrian's Wall in Britain, for example, separated much of the isles with a system of mounds, ditches, and stone walls. He created another such fortified border between Mainz (on the Rhine River) and Regensburg (on the Danube).

Portrait of the Emperor Antoninus Pius, who ruled AD 138–161

The Emperor Hadrian (AD 117–138), pictured in relief on the triumphal arch erected in Rome in his honor

Undermining the Vespasian reform whereby indigenous auxiliary military personnel served at a distance from home, he recruited locals to keep his confined armies at full strength. He blurred the distinction between auxiliary and legion-

The remains of Hadrian's triumphal arch at Eleusis, Greece. There Hadrian restored classical buildings, erected new ones, and was initiated into the Eleusinian Mysteries.

naires and between equites and senator insofar as legion officer rank was concerned. He conducted frequent personal inspections, spending most of his period of office traveling (AD 121–125 and 128–134). He visited all the provinces and virtually every city, intervening everywhere he went.

Hadrian also blurred civilian rank distinction, employing many equites in his civil service who had not been required to perform military duty. They began to replace freedmen in imperial household activities, including his own advisory council. This encroachment on functions tra-

ditionally carried out by the Senate, coupled with the fact that he gave it no say in the affairs of state, cost him support.

In private, Hadrian was an original man. He made beards the Roman fashion simply by not shaving. Something of an amateur architect, he had an enormous villa built for himself at Tivoli, just outside Rome, which broke all architectural rules of the time. He named its hall, courtyards, and gardens for sites he had visited on his travels. When a young man he loved, named Antinous, drowned in the Nile, the grief-stricken emperor deified him, founding the city Antinoupolis on that river in memorial.

Hadrian grew moody in his final years, plagued by disease and a frustrating search for a worthy heir. Having executed his only male relative in AD 136, he adopted one Lucius Ceonius Commodus (renamed Lucius Aelius Caesar), who died shortly thereafter. In AD 138, he adopted the Senator Titus Aelius Antoninus.

Antoninus Pius: A Reign of Quiet Prosperity (AD 138–161)

This senator of Gallic ancestry was confirmed by the Senate. His persuasion of the Senate to deify Hadrian is said to have earned him the name Antoninus Pius. He was 51 years old and childless. As requested by his predecessor, he had adopted two sons: Marcus Aurelius (nephew of his wife) and Lucius Verus (son of Hadrian's adopted son Lucius Caesar).

His was a peaceful reign, largely unaffected by the occasional border raids. He advanced Hadrian's frontiers in Britain (marked by the new Antonine Wall), in Dacia, and in the Rhineland. In AD 148, he celebrated the 900th anniversary of Rome. Not surprisingly, Antoninus was deified upon his death. Marcus Aurelius wrote: "My predecessor and adoptive father, Antoninus Pius, was a model of simplicity and perseverance, of disdain for hollow words, of diligence and resolve. He... respected the rights of all. I learned from him...to serve mankind unselfishly..."

Marcus Aurelius: Field Commander and Philosopher (AD 161–180)

Marcus Aurelius, successor to Antoninus, did just that, serving unselfishly. Wanting only to rule benignly over a peaceful people, he spent his time instead in border wars while disease ravaged the population. In his tent, the unhappy but dutiful emperor wrote his Meditations on his Stoic beliefs. He asked himself, "Are you satisfied, having done what nature demands of you, as if the eye would expect payment for looking and the foot a wage for walking?"

Aurelius made Lucius Verus his co-emperor (until Verus's death in AD 169). This was the first undermining of the unity of imperial power. Other events under Aurelius further presaged the end of the empire two hundred years later, particularly the recurring incursions along the frontiers and even into Italy by migrating Germanic peoples.

Almost as soon as Aurelius was in power, the Parthians grew restive again. The new princeps sent in his co-emperor and an army, under the command of the Syrian Avidius Cassius. With little assistance from Verus, the army succeeded in protecting the the imperial borders and client kingdoms in the east by AD 166. It also returned to Rome with the plague. In AD 175, Cassius declared himself emperor in the east. (Language may have played some part in his success here: he spoke Greek, like the majority of people in the east, as against the Latin of the west.) The rebellion he fomented lasted two years, until Cassius was murdered.

Finally able to turn his attention again to central Europe, Aurelius had hardly resecured the borders when he died in Vindobona (Vienna) in AD 180, leaving the empire to his nineteen-year-old son Commodus.

Provincial Government

By AD 180, despite the ominous events in Aurelius's reign, the concept of the principate introduced by Augustus was completely accepted, regardless of the occasional bad princeps. In the provinces particularly, any return to the old republican system of governance would have been impossible. It was an era of great prosperity: adopting the ways of Rome seemed the only sensible course.

As in the past, the Senate appointed ex-magistrates (entitled proconsul) as governors in the oldest, safest, and least important provinces. Strategically important provinces had their governors chosen by the princeps. (Egypt was even regarded as his personal property. Senators wishing to enter or to leave needed a special permit.) Only these imperial provinces, governed by ex-consuls called legates, were permitted to

In matters of war Hadrian pursued a policy of defense. A good example of this is Hadrian's Wall in the north of England, built as protection against invasions by the Picts.

base legions. In small provinces, the emperor would sometimes nominate government officials (called *procuratores*) from among the equites.

Governors did not go to their provinces

Relief on Marcus Aurelius's Column in Rome, depicting the emperor on a four-horse chariot. Following Trajan's example, Marcus Aurelius had this column erected to immortalize his war deeds.

alone. Each was followed by a retinue of lower officials. Governors were to ensure the smooth collection of taxes, to maintain law and order, and to function as judges, traveling throughout the provincial districts to the various cities where trials could be conducted. Some cities retained the privi-

lege of administering their own justice in minor cases without resort to the governor.

Provincial governors were paid salaries by this era but often added to them in a number of ways. Governors who had led an army had the right to allocate Roman citizenship, for example. This valuable asset was frequently for sale.

Despite all its injustice, the power of the emperors brought about unprecedented peace during the first two centuries after Christ. For the first time, trading could take place in safety from one end of the Mediterranean to the other. Large areas in the west and north were developed for the first time. Provincial products were sold throughout the empire. The new prosperity made rule by corrupt governors bearable, as it was not difficult to recover the money paid to them in fines and extortion.

Local Self-rule

Self-rule for the province dwellers had gradually developed under the principate system, especially in the west. Originally, all councils in the provinces had been little more than religious assemblies which gathered once a year in the temples of Rome and Augustus. In the provincial cities, on the other hand, political assemblies were increasingly allowed to flourish. Self-rule was ultimately granted to countless cities. Even from the very beginning, some cities (the *coloniae*, founded by Roman citizens in a conquered area) were granted a certain autonomy. There were also *municipia* (associated cities where Roman citizens had their own laws and magistrates), with rights and obligations established by treaty with Rome. Finally, there were the tributary cities, subjected to heavy taxes and given no special privileges.

Roman writers tell us very little about conditions in these various cities. Most were ruled by two magistrates called a *duumviri* (duovirate or "two men") whose authority was clearly based on the Roman consulate. They received no payment for their work. On the contrary, they were expected to give a huge banquet when nominated and to provide charity to the population out of their own pockets. Inscriptions in the streets of the excavated city of Pompeii indicate that the citizens were very interested in elections, not surprising if the candidates had to organize spectacular events to win votes. Under the duovirate were the aediles, in charge of public works. Quaestors were responsible for finances. Each city had a kind of senate, the *ordo decurionum*, filled with ex-govern-

The Angels' Castle (Castel Sant'Angelo) on the right bank of the Tiber in Rome was
Hadrian's monument.

Bust of the Emperor-philosopher Marcus Aurelius (AD 161–180), who published a number of books giving clear exposition of his principles

ment officials. The system appears to have worked well. The urban prosperity and energy of the era are evident in the imposing buildings constructed so well they still stand today.

Romanization

Any province where the degree of development could not match the achievements of Rome would be overwhelmed by Latin culture. This was invariably the case in the western provinces. Western aristocracies had often sided with the Romans and often quickly adopted their new master's culture. After a few attempts at rebellion, ordinary citizens usually gave up, as well. Gaul, the Iberian peninsula, and Dacia became so Romanized that the languages spoken there now are derived from Latin.

The army played a significant part in this Romanization, stationing legions in permanent army encampments to maintain order in strategically important provinces. As the legions were stationed at militarily sensitive points, the camps were always protected, surrounded by a moat and fortified walls. Towers were located at equal distances around the walls. Four gates opened at the ends of two main streets, the *cardo* and the *decumanus*, set at right angles to each other. Maps showing this structure have been found for many cities. Some camps were joined by a series of forts and walls, like those found in Britain and between the Rhine and the Danube.

Planned in a manner closely related to that of Roman cities, the camps themselves constituted actual towns, where farmers and tradesmen from all over the area came to sell their products. Legion soldiers were Roman citizens who had signed up for sixteen years. This guaranteed them a fixed salary and, as a pension, a farm in a border area or a sum of money. The six thousand soldiers who made up each legion lived in simple huts with their families, either inside or adjacent to an encampment. The legions laid roads, built bridges, drained marshes, dug canals, and built up their camp towns. All these grand works invited immigration and served as examples of Roman lifestyle, appealing to many peoples.

Detail of the sarcophagus (stone coffin) of one of Marcus Aurelius's generals, depicting a battle between Romans and barbarians

792

Hunters carrying their kill, a wild boar, back home. Detail of a mosaic from the Roman city of Casale

Life in Rome

City Life, Trade, and Marriage

Was Rome a pleasant city to live in? The intellectuals and writers did not necessarily think so, from what we can tell in surviving writings. Horace said he was always reluctant to visit the capital city. Juvenal, a poet who tried to make a living there, wrote thousands of bitterly critical verses about it. He hated his fellow citizens, the stench, the noise, the affectation.

The plan of the city itself was a problem. Virtually every emperor after Augustus tried to immortalize his name through the construction of impressive new buildings in Rome. Over three centuries, the city was given a facade of marble temples and palaces, theaters, *fora* (public squares), and colonnades.

Working-class residential areas spread out chaotically behind these, the *insulae* (unplanned blocks of poorly built apartment buildings) with which speculators had filled the city since it began. It was in these that the ordinary Roman had his small apartment. Thin walls separated him from his neighbors. Courtyards were never much more than shafts. Building collapse was common. The insulae were built so close to each other that the streets were never more than a few yards apart.

After the infamous fire in AD 64, Nero ordered more systematic reconstruction. He insisted on the use of brick-faced concrete, not wood, to improve fire resistance. He placed height limits on all new buildings

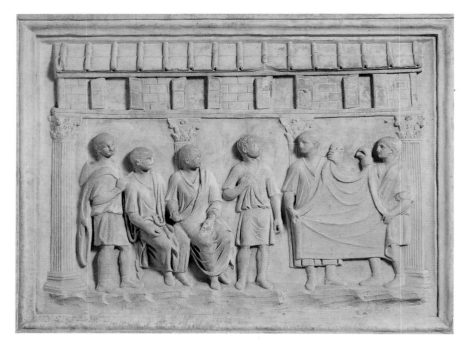

Interior of a fabric and cushion store in Rome. On the right, two customers sit on a small bench, with their slaves behind them, while the owner and his servants show their wares.

I.PACONIVS.T.F.COL.CALEDVS.
OCTAVIA.N.L.SALVIA.

A Roman farmer named Titus Paconius, according to the inscription, supervises the harvest, notebook in hand.

This shopping street, the Via Biberatica, was situated near the Forum (marketplace) built by the Emperor Trajan. In such streets the Romans did their daily shopping.

and he demanded wider streets.

All this did not help very much. Less than twenty years later, half the city went up in flames again. It is not surprising, as the Romans used torches and oil lamps for light. They cooked and heated on small earthenware stoves. Hardly an hour would go by without a fire somewhere. When one broke out, the fire brigade (initiated under Augustus) would be mobilized. Water had to be carried from the Tiber in buckets. It was frequently impossible to actually put out a fire. It would simply be contained until it burned itself out.

About a million Roman citizens crowded the narrow streets. Caesar had ordered that chariots were allowed in the streets only after sunset. This made for noisy nights. Once the vehicular traffic diminished, the human was still there, huge crowds of slaves and freemen, Romans and foreigners, children and adults. The wealthy, carried in sedan chairs, would force their way through the throngs.

The worst chaos was on the Argiletum, the most famous shopping street in the empire. It ended not far from the Senate building and the Forum Romanum, at one time the center of economic life. Various emperors had built new fora in the middle of the city. Trajan built multistory shopping galleries nearby his famous pillar. Unusually solid, these Markets of Trajan continued to be used by shopkeepers right up to this century.

Trade

The situation in Rome was not typical of the entire empire. We get a picture of a quieter and more monotonous life from writings about Alexandria and Antioch, smaller cities which formed the backbone of the empire. Although by the second century there was a great influx of immigrants to the cities, Romans were trad-

itionally a farming people. Even among the urban people, the ideal was to own a good piece of land and to work it themselves as necessary.

Farming was considered the most respectable profession, but when possible, the Romans used slaves or tenant farmers. Manual work of any other kind was lower caste. Those earning money by any other means would usually invest it in choice land with a villa on it, adopting the life style of the respectable person of independent means. For most Romans, however, owning land and a home remained a dream. Provincial inhabitants farmed small plots or served as tenant farmers for the rich. Rural or urban, the average Roman had little privacy and still less money.

City dwellers worked as craftsmen, shopkeepers, or general laborers. Many of these were freed slaves who had migrated to Rome in great numbers. They were enterprising, eager to try their hands at commerce, and willing to fight the social stigma against them. Some became equites; a few became quite wealthy. Traditional Roman *mercatores* (merchants), who were often equites, relied on their families to help them. Young sons or grandsons took care of their fathers' correspondence. The

The gay colors on the inside of this dish show a Roman carpenter, surrounded by his work.

795

lucky ones got rich. Yet the ideal remained the farmer.

Petronius wrote a story in Nero's time that illustrates this. He describes a certain Trimalchio, who began life as a slave. He won the trust of his master and was rewarded with a considerable inheritance and his freedom. With the money, Trimalchio was able to import wine from North Africa, which he was able to sell to Italian customers. He lost money, borrowed more, and stopped importing and selling wine as soon as he had enough money. By the end of his life, he was living on an estate on the Gulf of Naples, immensely wealthy, and

norm. Large companies with divided responsibilities did not fit with the trade legislation of the time. Roman law permitted such companies only if they leased certain state concessions. Even then, trading companies were limited in size and permitted only a single trading voyage over land or sea.

Between the Forum and the Tiber was a large and thriving trading district. Here, riches of all kinds were sold, transported to Rome by small ships from the harbor town of Ostia at the mouth of the Tiber. Tradesmen and bankers worked side by side. Artisans and craftsmen had their own district which stretched across the Forum. Booksellers, shoemakers, wool merchants, barbers, smiths, flaxworkers – all had a workplace there. Those with the same trade joined together in *collegia*, early forms of trade guild. Primarily social societies, they would help members in trouble but offered little else. They did function as burial societies: paid-up membership guaranteed a proper funeral.

Domestic Life

We know much more about the elite of Roman society than about the masses. This section examines domestic life from the point of view of the owner-occupiers of the better homes (*domus* in the city; *villa* outside).

As soon as a child was born, it would be placed on the floor in front of the house altar for the father to inspect. He had the right to accept the newborn baby – or to reject it. If he picked it up, this meant he accepted the child as his own. After eight or nine days, it would be given a name.

A cobbler at work in his shop, as shown on a sarcophagus found in Ostia, Rome's main port

not incidentally, able to lend money at high interest.

Trade was always conducted on a small scale. Because of a concept called *manus* (from the word for hand, connoting personal ownership or obligation), each merchant saw himself as responsible for his own actions. The single independent merchant trading at his own risk was the

Children were often entrusted to a wet nurse. Greek women were recognized as particularly good mothers, with the advantage that they could also teach Greek to the child at an early age. Poor hygiene and a wide variety of infectious diseases killed many infants and toddlers. If the child reached the age of six or seven, the parents would start thinking about school.

Marriage

Until they came of age, sons were formally under their fathers' authority. In former times, they could even be sold under the authority of the power called *manus* (ownership). Even after they came of age, sons could not by law own any goods. Over time, they were given more freedom. Augustus granted them access to money they earned in the army. Later, they were granted the right to possess goods inherited from the mother.

Roman lawyers spent a great deal of time investigating problems of ownership. They drew up a practical formulae for everything. Property legislation was even used to arrange adoptions.

Continuation of the family line was very important to Roman family men, part of the reason many of them had to resort to adoption. The Twelve Tables decreed that a man might only sell his son three times; the third time released him from manus. The manus itself could be sold. If a natural father sold his son to an adoptive father three times in front of a tribunal, the adoptive father could then set him free three times. This broke all of the son's bonds with his own family and put him under the manus of his new father.

Marriage was also a kind of purchase. The Romans had three types. Originally, only patricians were allowed to legally marry. This was the *confarreatio* (a word which means marriage by the ceremony of the cake). This was a religious ceremony in which both bride and groom ate cake. It placed the bride completely under the manus of her groom. Another type was the *coemptio* (which literally means purchase). This also placed the wife under the manus of her husband. Both forms fell into disuse many years before Augustus.

Only the third type of marriage kept the wife outside of her husband's manus. This kind, called *usus* (or use), only placed the wife under the manus of her husband after they had been living together uninterruptedly for a year. If she were to interrupt this year by staying out of the house for three nights in succession, she could avoid her husband's manus.

Stages in the life of a Roman child: on the left, the father watches him being fed by the mother, next he is carried on the father's arm. In the middle, he is riding a cart, and on the right he is following a lesson.

Part of a Roman mosaic with Cupid assisting during the wine harvest

Roman gold bracelet, necklace, and pins from the first century AD

However, a woman could never be totally independent. By law, she had no more freedom than a child, although in practice she often had a considerable latitude to act. If she were not under the manus of her husband, her father or guardian always possessed that power. Parental permission was always required for marriage. If the wed-

A ropemaker
at work in his shop.
Marble relief
on a sarcophagus
at Ostia

ding took place in accordance with usus, then the wife was allowed to be a guest in religious matters from then on.

A source of problems for Roman lawyers was the dowry, introduced so that the wife would contribute to family costs. It indicated that the union was more than just living together. In practice, the dowry caused big problems. Who should it be allocated to if the marriage broke up, for example? The judges filled volumes of jurisprudence on the subject. Divorces were very common, although there is no

reason to think that Roman marriages were any more or less happy than today's. Love softened many of the hard edges of legislation; few societies have honored women and mothers as much as the Roman. Many Roman women were buried in the same grave as their husbands. The gravestones were often engraved with the letters SUQ, for *sine una querella* (without a single argument).

Education

Roman schools were not very impressive. They were often run by discharged soldiers who earned a living from the tuition. Books were few and costly. Most things had to be learned by rote. Apart from basic reading and writing, pupils did not learn very much. The wealthy would frequently engage an educated slave (*pedagogue*) familiar with literature and philosophy. In Vespasian's day, the writings of Virgil, Lucan, and Horace were indispensable for schoolchildren. Greek masters placed great emphasis on Homer and Menander. Generally speaking, this is as far as education went. But some pupils went on to a school of rhetoric, where they were taught a form of history, useful in political debate. Here, the focus was on eloquence.

Up to the time of Vespasian, classes in rhetoric were set up only by private individuals, but he founded a state school for the purpose. Rhetoric was a formal art. The Alexandrian scholars had studied the discourses of the great Greeks in depth and had established criteria for ideal rhetoric, concentrating solely on style. Content was ignored. Latin scholars followed, turning eloquence into pure technique. The only courses that existed outside the schools of rhetoric were law studies. The result was that, apart from lawyers, the only academics were freed Greeks and Orientals.

Detail of a mosaic showing a four-horse chariot taking part in a race. The name of the charioteer can be seen above the horses' heads.

Bread and Games

Roman Leisure Activities

It was Juvenal who said that all the Roman people wanted was *panem et circenses* (bread and circuses or, by extension, games). Hundreds of thousands of people evidently agreed. For generations, the Roman emperors gave them both. Even in the time of the Republic, officials had tried to win popularity with grain handouts, enormous spectacles, and huge public sporting events.

The practice of grain distribution was rooted in the fact that the urban poor had very little steady work, owing to the limited opportunities open to them in commerce and industry. However, only about a quarter of the population qualified for handouts. The rest earned their own meager living. The custom took various forms over the centuries. Gaius Gracchus, for example,

initiated the sale of grain at fixed low prices. Under Clodius, this was changed to free handouts. The system was continued under the emperors as a way to satisfy their subjects.

A Year of Celebrations

The typical Roman year did offer ample opportunuties, however, for celebration. Political leaders could gain significant popularity by exploiting that fact. Some festivities dated from the time of the kings, mentioned in the calendar of the legendary King Numa. Others were instituted by the people in difficult times to appease the gods.

The *ludi magni* (or big games) dated from the year 217 BC, when Hannibal had threatened Rome's existence. Games honor-

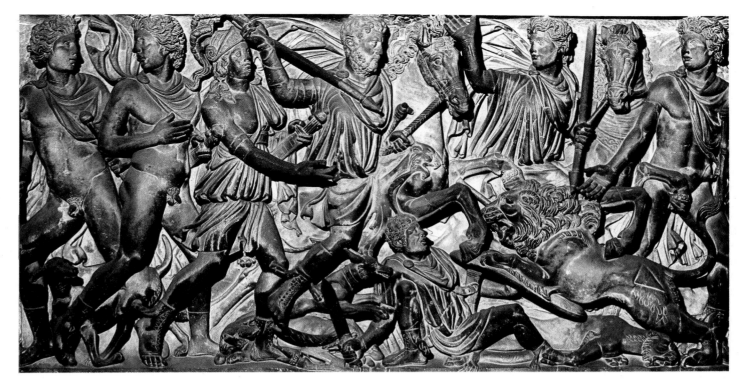

A lion in a fight with gladiators, as pictured on a Roman sarcophagus

Gladiator recruits got rough training in barracks under a strict military regime. This beautifully decorated helmet was found in the barracks at Pompeii.

ing Caesar and Augustus were initiated by their successors. In the era of the emperors, new celebrations were added continually. In the second and third centuries AD, the Roman year counted almost as many holidays as working days!

Each district had its own local guardian spirit. Its altar was the focal point of the annual festivities organized by the local residents in honor of that spirit. These festivals, originally religious in nature, gradually grew to such proportions that the state had to draw up rules for them.

Collegia

The government established rules, as well, for festivities organized by the *collegia* (guilds) of various trades. On the ninth of June, for example, the *collegium* of millers and bakers held their celebrations; on the thirteenth, the collegium of musicians held theirs. In both, drunken participants wandered through the streets. Statutes of a brotherhood of Diana and Antinous discovered in Lavinium, just outside Rome, reveal an official objective of worship and a practical interest in ensuring the members a decent burial as well as a good time. Each member paid an initial membership fee of twenty gold pieces and an amphora of good wine and, thereafter, an annual contribution of three gold pieces. The brotherhood, in return, provided a funeral for sixty gold pieces. A new chairman was appointed every five years. He did not have to do much except supervise the affairs of the club and organize a meeting six times a year. Every two months, the members met to see who could drink the most wine.

Some brotherhoods got involved in local politics, as well. "We don't want any Egyptian judges," is written on a wall excavated in the city of Pompeii, probably referring to the brotherhood devoted to the Egyptian goddess Isis, whose members had put themselves forward for the city council.

The Blood Games: Gladiators and Animals

Of all festivals, the blood games, or *ludi*, were most popular. There were three variations of combat: man to man, in which gladiators fought each other to the death; man to animal, in which wild animals were brought out to fight gladiators; and animal to animal.

All types were held in an amphitheater where the audience sat in tiered rows around an *arena* (which literally means "the sand"). Such stone amphitheaters were built on the Italian peninsula beginning with the late Republic. As the empire grew, more were built in virtually every province. One of the largest and most famous was the Colosseum in Rome.

Gladiatorial combat, like many Roman customs, had a religious background. The Etruscans, preceding the Romans on the Italian peninsula, had organized fights to the death between prisoners of war at the funerals of prominent men. The victims were intended as human sacrifices to the dead. The Romans adopted this practice about the third century BC, but the combats became a bloody spectator sport, a new and extremely popular form of mass entertainment. Schools were founded to train the gladiators. Games organizers - in the Republic, an offical; in the principate, the emperor himself - could order individual gladiators from these schools for particular performances. Originally, the combatants were prisoners of war, convicted criminals, or slaves rented or sold to the schools. This last category was banned by the emperors. By then, most of the gladiators were prisoners. There were also many volunteer gladiators passionately seeking the excitement and adventure or the riches a successful combatant could gain, despite the fact that most of them met a wretched death in the arena.

The audience enjoyed these bloody exhibitions, discussing the performances of the combatants and placing bets on the

Tragedies and comedies were performed in open-air theaters built on the Greek model. This Roman theater at Caesarea, in present-day Israel, is still used for stage and orchestral performances.

outcome. The gladiators were often costumed, dressed in beautiful suits of armor or as dreadful fishermen with nets and tridents. At the end of the fight, the victor would keep his opponent under control while the audience decided his fate. The victor would look up at the stands and wait. If the audience turned their thumbs down, it meant "weapons down' and the defeated man would be spared. Thumbs up meant "stab him." Seriously wounded gladiators were always finished off by special officials dressed as Charon, the mythical ferryman who bore the dead across the River Styx to the land of the dead. Victors, applauded in the arena, were rewarded with a sum of money and occasionally set free after a series of wins. The few lucky ones could live off their earnings for the rest of their lives or take up training other gladiators.

The average Roman saw nothing wrong with gladiatorial combat and even took his children to see it, thinking it a good thing for children to be confronted with violence at an early age. Only a few intellectuals were repelled by these exhibitions, usually not out of empathy, but because they found it boring or bad for the soul. Nobody pitied the gladiators themselves (after all, they were convicted criminals, or daredevils who only had themselves to blame), much less the animals.

The political leaders, republican and imperial alike, were expected to be there. In 55 BC, Pompey set a record: five days of games, involving the deaths of 500 lions and 50 elephants. Caesar and Marcus Aurelius went to the games but used the time to catch up on correspondence. Most of the other emperors, however, were thrilled by the games. Even Cicero enjoyed bloody fights between men and animals.

Martial, who wrote during Domitian's reign, devoted a whole volume of poetry to gladiatorial combat. St. Augustine, the church father, tells the story of a young Christian in the fourth century AD invited to go to the amphitheater. He agreed to go

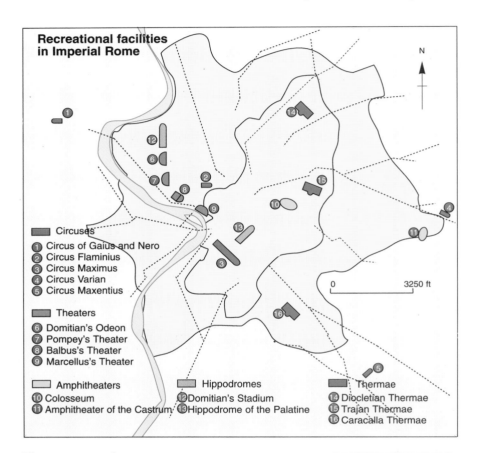

Recreational facilities in Imperial Rome

N

■ Circuses
① Circus of Gaius and Nero
② Circus Flaminius
③ Circus Maximus
④ Circus Varian
⑤ Circus Maxentius

■ Theaters
⑥ Domitian's Odeon
⑦ Pompey's Theater
⑧ Balbus's Theater
⑨ Marcellus's Theater

▢ Amphitheaters
⑩ Colosseum
⑪ Amphitheater of the Castrum

▢ Hippodromes
⑫ Domitian's Stadium
⑬ Hippodrome of the Palatine

■ Thermae
⑭ Diocletian Thermae
⑮ Trajan Thermae
⑯ Caracalla Thermae

0   3250 ft

There was extensive variety in the popular entertainment of Rome. The people could visit the thermae (public baths), circuses, or a stadium or a hippodrome to watch horse races.
They could go to the gladiator fights at the Colosseum or the Castrum amphitheater.
The ruins of most of these places can still be visited today.

This detail of a Roman mosaic from the third century AD shows gladiators fighting wild animals (including a lion, a gazelle, and an ostrich).

SABATIUS

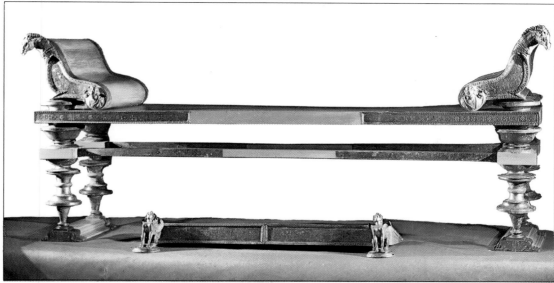

Roman bed
from the beginning
of the empire

but resolved to keep his eyes shut. The deafening roar of the crowd made him open them for a second - and from that moment on he found it impossible to take them off the bloody spectacle.

The games grew gradually bigger and bigger. Sometimes whole battles were performed, even mock naval battles in a flooded arena or on an artificial lake. There were even special amphitheaters for these, called *naumachiae*. The mock naval battles and the games involving exotic animals were the most expensive to stage.

Animal games took many different forms. There were fights between animals in odd combinations (for example, a bear versus a rhinoceros or a wild ox versus a lion). There were hunts, with trained hunters against wild animals, downed with arrows and spears while the audience applauded. Another version pitted animals against humans, with the human as victim: convicted criminals were given wooden sticks or were completely unarmed, sometimes even tied to a pole, and presented to starved beasts of prey or wild bulls. This was often the fate of Chritians condemned to death in the arena by the Roman authorities. Some executions were presented as myths or well-known stories. Human victims were sewn into the hides of animals and torn to pieces, for example, or forced to play the role of a famous person killed by wild beasts.

Their cost is one of the reasons that amphitheater games disappeared in the fourth and fifth centuries AD: the emperors would not pay to stage them anymore. Christianity was also having an influence, altering attitudes toward killing people in public spectacle; killing as entertainment was opposed by the church. Gladiatorial

combat was gradually made impossible in a world converting to Christianity. Public executions of convicted criminals, however, were still permitted, intended to serve as cautionary example.

The Lion's Den

The "lion's den" in the "Book of Daniel" in the *Old Testament* was meant literally, a reference to the Roman practice of putting men in arenas with wild lions. The sixth chapter of "Daniel" recounts Daniel's delivery from a den of lions. Much of the imagery in the rest of "Daniel" is derived

This fresco (mural painting), from Herculaneum, shows a banquet. The man is drinking wine while the woman holds out her hand toward the servant, who is bringing her something.

Pompeii and Herculaneum

The eruption of the volcano Mount Vesuvius, near Naples, is described in detail in one of the letters of the Roman writer, Pliny the Younger. It deals with the death of his uncle, Pliny the Elder, an important physicist who was the commander of a naval squadron in the Bay of Naples at the time of the eruption.

"Even though the mountain smoked ominously for a time, the inhabitants of the little towns on the slopes were barely concerned," he wrote. "They were pretty sure that the volcano was extinct. They did not connect the tremors they felt now and then to the impending disaster. One afternoon Pliny saw from his ship how the top of the mountain, as it were, exploded. Large gas clouds rose up from the crater. In Pompeii, it rained pieces of stone, the earth trembled and a large stream of lava started to crawl slowly down the mountain. Pliny went ashore to observe the phenomenon close up, but lost his life in doing so." The eyewitness report of his nephew goes on to

After the eruption, lava and ashes formed an envelope around the victims, within which the bodies decomposed. These casts of people in death agony provide a penetrating picture of the disaster.

describe how panic broke out when the people realized too late what was happening and tried to find safe shelter.

A few days later the three cities of Pompeii, Herculaneum, and Stabiae had disappeared from the earth. The thousands of dead provided sufficient warning never to rebuild the cities again. In the Middle Ages, there were only vague stories about a forgotten district called Pompeii. Farmers working the fruitful volcanic soil sometimes found a tile from a roof or pieces of pottery, but nobody attached any real value to them.

It was not until 1748 that Pompeii was discovered again. The king of Naples had a great interest in archaeology and ordered systematic digging carried out. Under the lava, the ash, and the mud, his workers discovered the entire city, with its many large houses, a forum with several temples, and a large theater. Behind the forum, they found an older part of the city with winding streets and shops.

The snapshot, so to speak, that Pompeii gives us provides a wealth of information about daily life in a provincial Roman city, including the bathing customs evident from the public baths near the Pompeii Forum. The walls of the houses, for example, contain all kinds of graffiti, from election slogans and advertising for a theater performance to declarations of love and children's rhymes. Complete working sites and entire households, with all the inhabitant's utensils, have been dug up. The frescoes discovered on the walls of many houses, a number of which are shown in this book, form one of the few sources of knowledge of Roman painting.

Roman wall painting is especially remarkable for its illusionism and architectural fantasies. This was vital to the development of Renaissance painting and decoration.

View of the ruins of Pompeii, with Vesuvius in the background. Archeologists are still excavating the remains of the entire city.

from Mesopotamian and Persian mythology; this one rests on Roman reality.

The book of Daniel was probably written as a parable to illustrate the benefits of faith to the Jews oppressed during the middle of the second century BC by the Seleucid King Antiochus IV. It details the story of a youth clinging to his faith in spite of great obstacles. Several fragments of the book were found in the Dead Sea Scrolls discovered in caves near Qumran, Jordan, in 1947.

Chariot Races
The Roman people's second passion was racing. Each city had its own racetrack, or *circus.* The Circus Maximus, lying between the Palatine and Aventine Hills in Rome, used from 600 BC to the sixth century AD, was known throughout the empire. At the

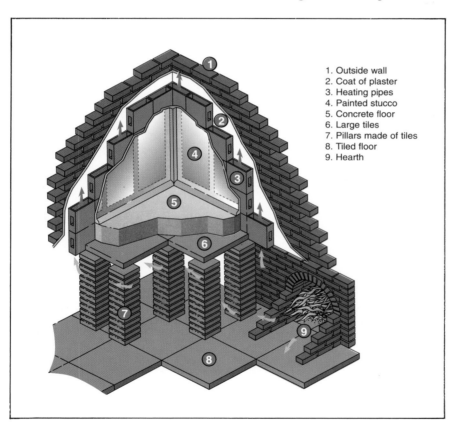

1. Outside wall
2. Coat of plaster
3. Heating pipes
4. Painted stucco
5. Concrete floor
6. Large tiles
7. Pillars made of tiles
8. Tiled floor
9. Hearth

The Romans heated their houses and baths by means of the hypocaustum system. This was a form of hot-air heating in which heat from a stoked fire in the cellar rose through hollow spaces under the floor and through pipes in the walls.
The pipes were covered with a coat of plaster, which in turn, was covered with a coat of beautifully painted stucco (fine, decorative plaster).

height of its popularity, in the second century AD, it could accommodate 250,000 spectators. Three tiers of seats surrounded an arena 1850 feet long (564 meters) and 280 feet (85 meters) wide, except for the stall at one end for horses and chariots. A low wall, the *spina* (spine), ran down the middle. Racing horses and chariots ran around it.

The chariot races were traditionally a religious spectacle, dedicated to the gods. Each race day in Rome started with the solemn procession of icons around the

circus, while the official who had organized the event was dressed up as Jupiter. The masses loved the races. Each race consisted of seven laps, in which four or more chariots took part. As many as 24 races could be held in a day. Each driver wore the colors of the circus school or party to which his horses belonged: green, blue, red, or white. Under the later emperors, only green and blue were used, and the audience was divided into groups of supporters for each of these colors. The emperors were expected to pick a color. This made the race more exciting.

The jockeys were usually young freedmen. The chariots had four horses (only the middle two actually pulled), sometimes more. The driver was strapped to his horses. If he fell, he had to cut the straps to survive. Injuries and fatal accidents were common; chariots often crashed into each other. The jockeys hung amulets around

their necks and on their horses and used incantations to summon demons against their opponents. Emperors were always present at the races to receive the cheers of the crowd and show themselves at one with the people. Racetracks were typically built close to the palace so that the emperor and his retinue could go directly to his box.

Changes in the Theater

During the empire, theaters existed together with the circuses and amphitheaters. They could also accommodate large numbers of people, but the masses were less interested in the stage than in spectacle. The Theater of Marcellus in Rome (from the time of Augustus) could accommodate 20,000 people, no match for the Colosseum with its 50,000 or the Circus Maximus (250,000).

Greek theaters were built into hillsides whereas Roman theaters were freestanding. Early Roman theaters were temporary structures. Anything more permanent was considered unnecessarily slothful. The first stone theater in Rome was built by Pompey. To justify his permanent theater, Pompey built a temple at the top of the theater, dedicated to Venus Victrix, his protectress divinity. Pompey filled his theater and its gardens with booty from the Greek east, creating a monument to Roman might and power, and to himself, Pompey the Great.

Artistic creativity faded as audiences appeared interested only in the grand achievements of their predecessors. Theatrical performances consisted of endless repeats, which the public watched in order to compare the talents of the actors. By way of variety, directors increased the role of the chorus. The *canticum*, the sung text, overshadowed the rest of the play and took on popular appeal. (When Ceasar's body

The large public baths usually had a library, as well as facilities for teaching. This relief shows a classroom scene.

807

was cremated in the forum, for instance, the watching crowd sang a famous canticum.) Eventually mime developed. The leading actor performed the play without words, to the sound of the music and the canticum. The ability of actors to perform scenes using only their hands was much admired. From these origins, opera and ballet developed. The Roman tragedy, as handed down by Seneca, was another variation. This type of play was nothing more than a monologue, presented by the author to his friends.

Roman married couple on a mural painting from Pompeii. The husband has a scroll in his hand.
The woman holds a slate covered with wax and a slate pencil, which was used as a writing instrument.

Lucius Annaeus Seneca, one of the most famous playwrights of Latin literature, was born about 4 BC in Córdoba, Spain, the son of the Roman rhetorician Marcus (Lucius) Annaeus Seneca, known as Seneca the Elder. At once a writer, a philosopher, and a statesman, Seneca the Younger, as he was known, studied first at the side of his father and later in Rome. He continued the family interest in rhetoric (the effective use of words, primarily in speacking), but was also strongly influenced by Stoic philosophy, eventually retiring to devote himself to its study and commentary on its doctrines, writing on such subjects as anger and peace of mind.

Stoicism

The Stoic school of philosophy that so captivated Seneca's attention was established around 300 BC in Athens by Zeno of Citium (on the island of Cyprus). The name comes from the *Stoa Poikile* (painted porch) where he held his classes.

The philosophy was introduced to Rome over a hundred years later by Panaetius of Rhodes. One of his students was Posidonius of Apamea (in Syria), a teacher of the Roman orator Marcus Tullius Cicero. Seneca was one of the three Stoic philosophers of the Roman Empire whose writings have survived. The others are Epictetus and the Emperor Marcus Aurelius. Stoicism was the most influential philosophy in the empire of their time. It played a crucial role in the concept of natural law underlying all Roman legal theory.

The Stoics were primarily concerned with the study of ethics, using theories of logic and natural science to support their conclusions. They held that reality is material, but that passive matter is distinct from the active principle, Logos, or divine reason, manifested in the human soul. The Stoics believed that loving according to nature or reason is living in conformity with the divine order of the universe. Because everything that happens is the result of divine will or, in any case, is outside one's control, a person should be calmly accepting of all happenings, free of such emotions as passion or grief, or even joy. Good is seen existing within the state of the soul itself, in the calm acceptance that constitutes wisdom, restraint from the passions and desires of daily life. The four virtues of Stoicism are wisdom, courage, justice and temperance. This classification was drawn from Plato.

It was perhaps the cosmopolitan nature of Stoicism that made it most attractive to the Romans, given their vast empire. All human beings are seen as manifestations of a single universal spirit and should, as such, live in brotherly love and equality. Race and rank are external differences of no importance in genuine social relationships.

Seneca is considered perhaps the most important Stoic philosopher of Rome. The characters in his plays exhibit Stoic fatalism and introspective natures. His tragedies, written in verse and adapted from Greek legends, were revived during the Renaissance and were influential in the later classical drama of Europe. He wrote voluminously on many subjects, many of which are lost. Existing writings include the *Quaestiones Naturales* (Natural Ques-

tions), dealing with meteorology and astronomy, and the *Apocolocyntosis Divi Claudi* (Pumpkinification of the Divine Claudius), a satire on the deification of the Emperor Claudius.

Seneca was well acquainted with Claudius, who appointed him tutor to his adopted son, the infamous Nero, in AD 49. Nero became emperor in 54. The moderate policies of his first years in office are attributed to the guidance he received from Seneca and his other major advisor, Sextus Afranius Burrus, commander of the Praetorian Guard. By 62, the emperor had changed his views on the now-wealthy philosopher and tried, without success, to have Seneca poisoned. In 65, Seneca, himself implicated in a conspiracy to kill Nero, committed suicide by imperial order.

Poetry and Oratory

The rich and well-educated spent much of their time attending recitals of various types: tragedy in the style of Seneca, his-torical pieces, or poetry. If the host considered himself a poet, some guests thought such an evening endless torture. Pliny the Younger remarks at one point that, "This year (AD 97) has brought us a fine crop of poets; during the month of April we had a reading by one or other poet almost every day. Most of the invited guests stay in the foyer, chatting, and only go in toward the end, hoping against hope that the author has finished."

Even Seneca himself declared his loath-ing for these men of letters. "The speaker appears holding a couple of sheets of paper covered in tiny letters. After he has read most of the manuscript, he asks, 'Would you like me to continue?' And the same people who wished he would suddenly drop dead, scream, 'Go on, go on!'"

Occasionally, poetry competitions were held in Rome and other cities. The juries were made up of priests, not always the greatest experts. Not much is known of the winning poets.

Reconstruction of a Roman kitchen, showing various utensils used at the time

We know that Florus, who published several small works in the time of Hadrian, was once refused a prize. The audience revered him most of all, he writes, but the emperor did not want to reward him, as he was not a pure Roman.

The Baths

Roman cities were dirty, dusty, and hot. Like the Hellenistic kings in the east, Rome built public baths for its citizens. These developed into community centers, where people met socially, bathed, swam, had a massage, or performed gymnastic exercises. There were even opportunities to study, as there was often a well-stocked library located in the bath complex. The baths found in Pompeii, dating from 75 BC, exhibit the extensive dressing rooms and facilities for cold, warm, and hot bathing typical of that era. They are no match for the huge marble-lined vaulted Baths of Caracalla in Rome, built in AD 217, with their space for 1600 bathers, their swimming pools, exercise facilities, lounges, and lecture halls.

The Romans baths of Aquae Sulis (Bath, England) were built in the 2nd century AD. This is a view of the large bath, that was reconstructed in the 19th century. The basin and the floors are original, including the base of the columns.

Ground plan of the Baths of Caracalla in Rome:
1. Cold bath (*frigidarium*);
2. Tepid bath (*tepidarium*);
3. Hot bath (*caldarium*);
4. Swimming pool (*natatio*);
5. Open air gymnasiums (*palaestra*).

N

Entrance

0   50 metres

Decline in Power

The Crisis in Roman Society

Toward the end of the second century, the Roman Empire slid into great crisis. Commerce and industry declined, fostering urban decay and political chaos. Agriculture deteriorated, leading to poverty and unrest even in the once flourishing provinces. Problems of renewed invasion, civil war, and economic ruin would contribute to finishing off the empire in less than a hundred years.

Commodus:
The Imperial Gladiator (AD 180–192)

Many of these problems were rooted in the era of the adopted (Antonine) emperors, although that period itself seemed one of great prosperity. Any remedial action that might have been undertaken to avert disaster was certainly not provided by the last of that line, Commodus, the profligate son of Marcus Aurelius. His rule itself was a disaster. Like that of Nero before him, he came to the emperorship very young and managed it so terribly as to be cursed by the Senate, receiving the *damnatio memoriae* (the removal from official record of his reign).

Nominally coemperor with Marcus Aurelius at the age of sixteen, Commodus inherited the empire at nineteen. The intent had been to train him for the position, but the young man had paid little attention to his lessons.

As emperor, and before, Commodus was interested only in seeking his own pleasure. Powerful and possibly paranoid, he lived in constant fear for his life, killing off anyone he suspected. He left the work of the empire to a collection of his favorites so he could enjoy himself in Rome. (They enjoyed themselves, too, with real-life games of intrigue, treason, and murder.)

The emperor's particular hobby was gladiatorial combat. He loved to watch it and, even more, to participate. Dressed as Hercules, Commodus would perform in person in the amphitheater, winning, of course, every time.

He made the Senate officially recognize him as a god. His play would lead to his death. On New Year's Eve in AD 192, just preceding his planned assumption of the consulate dressed as a gladiator, conspirators bribed his regular wrestling partner to strangle him.

Commodus ignored foreign policy and the plans of his father to expand the empire in central Europe. The frontiers held only because of the capabilities of the provincial governors and the land grant and settlement arrangements Aurelius had made with leaders on the Danube.

The Sale of the Emperorship

On New Year's Day, AD 193, the assassins of Commodus put forward Publius Helvius Pertinax, Prefect of Rome, as emperor. Although respected in the Senate, Pertinax, a nonaristocrat, had neither army nor wealth. His refusal to pay financial tribute to the praetorians led to his death. They murdered him at the end of March, AD 193.

Sulcipianus, a wealthy senator, then offered the praetorians 20,000 sesterces each for the throne. This donativum (a donation given to each praetorian on the emperor's accession) had become a common practice. His colleague, the aging General Didius Severus Julianus, outbid him, offering each 5,000 sesterces more. Satisfied praetorians escorted Julianus to the Senate. It could do nothing but confirm his nomination. The principate had become a commodity. Three powerful provincial armies abruptly challenged the action and the authority of Julianus, beginning the civ-

The Emperor Caracalla (AD 211 – 217) dreamed about following the example of Alexander the Great in his conquest of the east, even imitating the way his idol dressed.

The Emperor Septimius Severus (AD 193 – 211) with his spouse, Julia Domna, and his sons, Caracalla and Geta. The latter's head has almost totally disappeared.

il war of AD 193. Julianus was abandoned by his praetorians and beaten to death.

The Severi: Septimius Severus (AD 193–211)

First to hear of the praetorian purchase and nearest to Rome was the provincial army of the Danube. It declared Lucius Septimius Severus emperor in May, AD 193.

In Syria, the legate Pescennius Niger was put forward by his troops; while in Britain, Clodius Albinus was nominated by his.

Severus declared Albinus Caesar (the title designating an heir apparent to the throne), thus coopting him, but only for a while.

Severus then attacked and defeated Niger (despite that general's Parthian support in Mesopotamia), killing him in AD 194.

Two years later, Albinus, who had been busy earning support from the people and the Senate, in addition to what he already had from his soldiers, announced himself as Augustus (a title implying a share in imperial power). He proceeded to invade Gaul, where he was killed in February, AD 194. Severus destroyed his headquarters camp at Lugdunum (Lyons).

Imperial power in fact, not simply in name, now belonged to Severus. He would have to fight for it again in Mesopotamia and, later still, in Britain, defending Hadrian's Wall. He fell ill and died in Eburacum (present-day York, England) during a campaign against the Picts in AD 211.

Severus returned to Rome in AD 202. The new emperor came from the city of Leptis Magna, near Tripoli in north Africa, where he belonged to a Romanized family of provincial aristocracy. He had held both political office (including senator) in Rome and in the provinces and successful military command.

In AD 180, Severus had married the Syrian Julia Domna, daughter of the ruler of Emesa, the holy city central to the sun cult. Julia Domna's father was a high priest in the temple of Baal, associated with the sun. She herself, beautiful and intelligent, exerted great influence on her husband and children, her sister Julia Maesa, and her nieces, Julia Soemias and Julia Mammaea.

Together, the four eastern princesses formed a powerful clique in the emperor's court. Despite his age and his gout, Severus

Ruins of the city of Leptis Magna in North Africa, where Septimius Severus was born

813

Ruins of Caracalla's Thermae as seen in Rome today. In Imperial times, these formed a great architectural monument, decorated with pictures of gods, athletes, and benefactors.

traveled from border to border with his wife, significantly visiting his place of birth.

Severus also sought western influence, defining the stated direction of his administrative policy by declaring that he was the true son of the popular Marcus Aurelius. He even named his son Marcus Aurelius Antoninus, seeking connection with the Antonine dynasty.

His policy was, in fact, quite different from that of Aurelius. As emperor, his focus was provincial, not aristocratic. Severus never forgot his roots in the army of the Danube. He built a triumphal arch with three gates on a corner of the Forum Romanum to glorify his campaign against the Parthians. He built a similar arch in Leptis Magna.

More importantly, Severus used his mili-

tary and provincial concerns as the basis of a new social order dominated by equestrians. He placed Danubian elite in control of the Praetorian Guard, put three new legions under equestrian command, and established thousand-soldier auxiliary units in infantry and cavalry. He opened careers, both military and civilian, to the lower classes.

This was the Severan revolution. It extended to all matters of administration. He cut back on the privileges of the peoples of the Italian peninsula as he increased those of easterners and Africans, recruiting the latter for the first time for financial and government posts.

Severus's main interest, however, was law. He appointed Papinian, a famous lawyer commissioned to systematize the law, as Praetorian Prefect. This gave him not only significant power but the opportunity to implement his own insights and involve his office with the administration of justice.

Caracalla: Extravagant Tyrant (AD 211–217)

Severus had intended his two sons, then in their early twenties, to rule jointly on his death. However, within a year, Caracalla had his brother Geta put to the sword in the arms of their mother, Julia Domna. Caracalla ranks with Caligula, Nero, and Commodus as a megalomaniacal tyrant. He considered himself a god, because, he insisted, his father had ascended to the sun. In personal behavior, he was violent and debauched.

Yet in a reign characterized by extravagance and execution, he nevertheless continued the egalitarian social policies and the judicial and legislative changes begun by his father. He retained most of the individuals who had been advanced under his father.

In AD 212, through the *Constitutio Antoniniana de Civitate* (the Antonine Constitution of Citizenship), he conferred Roman citizenship on all free inhabitants of the empire. While it recognized a trend toward broader social empowerment that had been developing for some centuries, Caracalla probably did this for financial reasons. Certain taxes were only paid by Romans. This diminished the status of citizenship and the incentive it had offered to local people to join the military.

Economics was not his strong point. He increased the pay of ordinary soldiers, despite a shrinking treasury. He started an extensive building program that rapidly used up the vast fortune he had inherited. (It includes the expensive baths built in Rome whose ruins still bear his name.) To defray construction costs, he increased taxes on senators and doubled inheritance and emancipation taxes (paid by manumitted or freed slaves).

Using Alexander the Great as his model, Caracalla undertook to win the east. In mid-invasion in Syria in April, AD 217, he was murdered by the order of the Equestrian Praetorian Prefect Marcus Opellius Macrinus.

Macrinus (AD 217–218)

Unaware of Macrinus's role in the fate of their commander, Caracalla's soldiers hailed him as emperor. The Senate confirmed him, although he was an eques, the first to achieve such standing.

Head of a gladiator on a mosaic from Caracalla's Thermae.

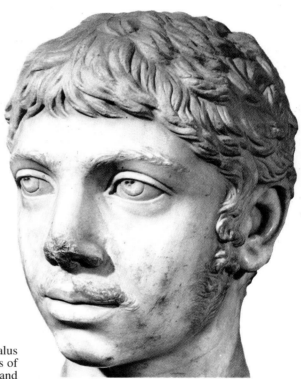

The Emperor Elagabalus (AD 218 – 222) left affairs of state largely to his mother and grandmother while he devoted himself completely to worshipping and idolizing the sun god Baal.

He completed Caracalla's objective of bringing Mesopotamia under Roman authority, but did it by financial arrangement, paying the Parthians. This was in keeping with his own background in finance. In a move for popularity, he also reduced the military budget and cancelled the taxes his predecessor had implemented.

The princesses at the court of Septimius

815

Severus did not stand idly by. They had the troops in Syria acclaim Bassianus, the son of Julia Soemias and grandson of Julia Maesa, as emperor. (The influential Julia Domna, widow of Severus, had died.) Since the boy was only fourteen, the women could retain their power for the time being. Macrinus and his own son (already on the throne with him) were killed right afterward.

Elagabalus: Debauched Emperor (AD 218–227)

The boy, Bassianus, had been brought up in his grandfather's temple, at the foot of the statue of Baal. He was, therefore, called El-a-Gabal, son of Baal, which the Romans changed to Elagabalus (or Heliogabalus). Presented to the Senate as the son of Caracalla, he also took the name Marcus Aurelius Antoninus. The young emperor was a remarkable sight, appearing in the palace in costume as the high priest of the sun god.

There are many stories about Elagabalus that may be exaggerated as we are unable to confirm them with reliable historical sources. For example, it is reported he led sensual dances prescribed by the rites of Baal, in addition to amazing processions through the streets.

Elagabalus wanted the whole empire to serve Baal, building a temple of worship to his god in Rome and spending enormous sums of money on sacrifices and religious ceremonies. The stunned Romans watched in disgust. When he had an ancient statue of the virgin goddess Vesta dragged to the Baal temple, perhaps trying to symbolize an integration of western and eastern cults, there was a huge outcry. He was marrying a Vestal virgin, committing sacrilege in the eyes of the Romans. Bizarre stories about his orgies spread through the city. Animosity toward him grew. After four years, the Praetorian Guard murdered him and set his cousin Alexianus in his place.

Alexander Severus (AD 222–235)

Another emperor at age fourteen, this one took as his example and his name Alexander the Great. Son of Julia Mammaea (the

Statue of the Syrian
sun god Baal, also called Helios
by the Romans.
The idolization of this god by
Emperor Elagabalus
was at first regarded favorably
by the Romans but later
with disgust.

sister and niece of Julia Domna), the latest boy-princeps had a different character than his immediate predecessors. Serious and docile, he had high regard for the office of emperor. He paid homage to his parents every morning in the *lararium*, the room containing statues of the house spirits. It is suggested that he also worshipped Alexander, Orpheus, Abraham, and even Jesus there, an indication of the mixture of religious ideas popular at that time.

It is difficult to say whether or not Alexander Severus would have been a good princeps. The *consilium principis* (or emperor's crown council, on which lawyers and senators sat) gained great influence during his reign. A new series of attacks on the Roman Empire intervened. The emperor, poorly suited to the role of warrior, saw it as his duty to go into battle. His mother, Julia Mammaea, who had always been his support and refuge, went with him, although she could do little for him in a general's tent. Following a defensive war in the east, the princeps had to travel to the Rhine where there were threats of invasion. In AD 235, during an argument with a group of soldiers at Moguntiacum (present-day Mainz), he and his mother were killed, ending the Severan dynasty.

Disintegration of the Empire (AD 235–285)

Maximinus, an unschooled officer from Thrace, reluctantly succeeded as emperor, under pressure from his soldiers. The year began a period of frequent wars and civil unrest. Between AD 235 and 285, no fewer than 26 emperors were appointed. Only one died a natural death. Fifty years later, with order restored, the Roman Empire had been altered radically.

In AD 235, the new princeps himself was rarely recognized in the empire. Rivals from one province or another constantly threatened his power. It was threatened in the south by desert people and, in the east, by the Persians who had brought Parthian rule to an end and inflicted heavy defeats on the Roman army.

Attacked in the north by Germans, Maximinus restored the safety of the Rhine border. In the provinces along the Danube, the main foes were the Goths, Germanic people from the coast of the Baltic. Tempted by the rich provinces of the Balkans and Asia Minor, the Goths dared to challenge the power of the Roman Empire. Their bands plundered Greece and their ships pillaged the Black Sea.

Another Germanic group, the Heruli,

Many Romans were what we would call superstitious. This second-century AD Roman mosaic from Antioch pictures all kinds of magic symbols, grouped around a magic or evil eye.

spread death and destruction along the coasts of the Aegean, and even ancient Athens. These primitive Germans might have felt out of place among the stone temples and urban riches of the east, but everything fell for a time to the power of their swords. Only in the sixties and seventies of this turbulent century would they be driven back by the emperors.

The Soldier-Emperors

In AD 235, major landowners in North Africa joined the Senate in rebellion against Maximinus, with his attitudes of antipathy to the educated clases and the Senate. The Thracian emperor was killed by his own army.

The Senate first established joint civilian control under Pupienus and Balbinus and then replaced it with the military man Gordian III. He was the first of several able soldier-emperors to follow each other in rapid succession.

Gordian III held power for five years, murdered in AD 244 by Philip the Arabian, an Arab (rumored to be a secret Christian) who had made a career in the Roman army. Philip made peace with the Persians by ceding part of the empire to them and paying cash tribute. His fabulous victory

Detail of a third-century ornament showing a fight between a Roman soldier on horseback and a number of barbarians

Remains of the
amphitheater built by
the Romans at Thysdrus,
present-day El Djem
in Tunisia

celebration in Rome coincided with the city's thousandth anniversary. The Roman people wanted to believe that a period of peace and prosperity had begun, but Philip's assassination proved it not the case.

Decius, the next princeps, in an effort to reimpose Roman custom, tried to eradicate the eastern religions, including Christianity, which had infiltrated even the imperial residence. He seized all church property and demanded a declaration of loyalty from his subjects, compelling them to make sacrifices to the gods of state in front of official witnesses. Many Christians, refusing to comply, died for their convictions.

Decius's attack was a heavy blow. Since the time of Marcus Aurelius, Christians had generally been left in peace, winning converts even in the highest Roman circles. Now, many of these new believers re-

nounced their faith rather than die as martyrs. In AD 251, Decius left for Dacia, planning to defeat the Goths. Instead, he and his entire army walked into a Goth ambush near the Black Sea and were killed.

Valerian and Gallienus (AD 253–268)

Two Roman senators, father and son, took over the emperorship. The father, Valerian, took particular interest in Christian persecution. Three years later, he was taken prisoner by the Persian King Shapur I, dying in captivity in AD 260, an unprecedented humiliation for a Roman princeps.

Disintegration and Recovery

Gallienus, making no move to alter his father's fate, continued the reign on his own. He halted the persecution of Christians, even returning their churches and graveyards. That fact and his own preference for the ancient Greek cult of Deme-

819

ter earned him powerful enemies among the traditionalists of the Roman elite. He also diminished senatorial influence, especially in the army, giving the preponderance of military command and provincial governorships to the equites. He developed a new corps and an agile cavalry in the army.

After a number of campaign victories on the Rhine and the Danube, consolidating what was left of his power, he found his

Mask of a Roman mummy, representing a very realistic portrait of the deceased, from a sarcophagus at El Fayum in the Roman province of Egypt

resources stretched too thin to act as new governments arose in Gaul and Palmyra. While in Mediolanum (modern Milan) dealing with the usurper Aureolus, he was murdered by his own officers.

Gaul

In AD 259, legions in Gaul, after a victory over the Germanic Franks, appointed their own commander Marcus Cassianius Postumus as princeps. Initially recognized only in Gaul (later in Spain and Britain), Postumus, realizing he had little chance of ruling the whole empire, established a government in exile in Augusta Treverorum (present-day Trier), complete with a senate and annual consuls. He issued his own coins and maintained his own praetorian guard. The situation held stable for eight years until Postumus was killed by his own rebelling soldiers. He was followed by the Gaul Tetricus, governor of Aquitania, who lacked the military background to be taken seriously by the army.

Palmyra

In AD 260, the desert city of Palmyra became the center of a virtually independent kingdom under Odaenathus. Roman Emperor Gallienus had given him free hand to maintain law and order and keep the Persians at bay. The people of Syria organized their own guerrilla bands to assist Odaenathus, who ultimately defeated the Persians near Carrhae. Although he began to call himself the king of Palmyra, Odaenathus never attempted to take over as emperor, nominally recognizing the authority of Gallienus in Rome. He proved to be a gifted ruler. Gallienus could do nothing but approve, giving him first the title Imperator and later "Inspector of all the East." Odaenathus was murdered about AD 268. His widow, Zenobia, immediately took control of key positions, had her son Vaballath handed his father's titles, and began an independent eastern monarchy in the Persian style. While the emperors in Rome had their hands full with barbarian invasions, Zenobia occupied Egypt and Asia Minor.

The Illyrian Emperors: Claudius II (AD 268–270)

In AD 268, Claudius II was set in power by the officers who had assassinated his imperial predecessor Gallienus. Extraordinarily successful in his efforts against the German peoples the Alamanni and the Goths, Claudius II died of the plague in AD 270.

The Illyrian Emperors: Aurelian (AD 270–275)

The capable soldier Aurelian took over the emperorship, routed the invading Juthungi (Goths) and Alamanni (Germans), and con-

Mosaic showing a ship anchored in a harbor. On the left is a picture of the harbor lighthouse.

structed a rampart (Aurelian's Wall) to protect Rome. He evacuated Dacia, determining it too difficult to defend. However, he defeated and captured the popular Queen Zenobia in AD 272.

In a second campaign, Aurelian went on to pillage Palmyra and seize Alexandria. He then went after Tetricius in Gaul, who offered little resistance when the princeps restored Roman rule in AD 274.

On the domestic front, Aurelian attempted to strengthen the currency by minting coins of more acceptable value and stopped riots in the mints themselves. To

Ruins of a Roman temple at Palmyra, which was ruled by Queen Zenobia during the reign of Emperor Gallienus (AD 253 – 268)

deal with the problems of food distribution in Rome, he put food providers (for example, bakers and meat sellers) under military authority.

It is his religious policy, however, that is most notable. In the interest of moral authority and personal power, he declared himself the chosen one of the *Sol Invictus* (Invincible Sun), to whom he designated a new temple. His occasional title *dominus et deus* (master and god) has been used to distinguish this new era Dominate from the old Principate.

Aurelian restored Roman authority throughout the empire but eventually he, too, was murdered by a group of officers. He was followed by a series of six competent generals over a nine-year period who continued in his style, purging the empire of invaders and revolutionaries.

Silver dish from Aquileia, with scenes glorifying agriculture

The Late Empire

New Structures

By the third century, the Roman Empire was staggering, its traditional political and social order undone, its army unable to perform its protective function, and its once thriving economy in ruins. What brought this about?

The Myth of Decadence

Popular opinion frequently ascribes the fall of the Roman Empire to the widespread general decadence in its final years. This is a myth which greatly oversimplifies the real situation. Complaints about the moral decay and the decline of the empire were first expressed in Cato the Elder's day, five hundred years before its actual end. In fact, such comments were historically commonplace. Christians carried on the criticism, proclaiming the disasters which struck the empire in the fourth and fifth centuries to be God's punishment for the sins of the wicked. While the notion of decadence has persisted, historians have found that the sto-

This Roman relief shows a donkey tied to a yoke, turning the millstone.

ries describing it are based primarily on those told by the Romans at the peak of the empire. Hardly typical of the population at large, they detail juicy tidbits about the private lives of their emperors. Like much of present-day journalism, they also tend to focus on abuses of the public trust. Imperial extravagances, like those of Caligula or Elagabalus, for instance, cannot be regarded as representative of the whole society. The vast majority of the population was poor, quite incapable of staging any great orgies.

The Role of the Army
Change within the army was a factor in the great crisis of the third century, according to the historian Tacitus. The black year of AD 69–70 had shown that the secret of

imperial power lay in its support by the legions outside Rome. If they remained loyal, an emperor could rule; if they rejected him, his reign was over. Each legion developed its own individual character and esprit de corps which depended on its location and composition as much as its military success.

Permanent legion encampments eventually developed into virtual small cities, drawing soldiers from the province in which they were stationed, and extending citizenship to them. In addition, the Roman army recruited large numbers of provincial noncitizens as auxiliary forces. After twenty-five years of service, they would be granted Roman citizenship. By the third century, even the auxiliary forces were made Roman citizens, virtually indistinguishable from the legions.

All troops at the time were recruited from border areas far from Rome and the Italian peninsula. They no longer felt strongly linked to the center of the empire and its culture. Foreigners were also increasingly recruited for the army to fight such invaders as Arabs, Iranians, and Germans. This tended to weaken the solidarity between soldier and empire.

Typical soldiers were loyal only to their own legions and generals. Even that could change. Generals often allowed plundering to provide for their troops. Postumus was killed by his own soldiers when he refused to allow them to plunder the city of Moguntiacum. During the third century, the general population was victimized as frequently by marauding legionaries as by invading barbarians.

There was an economic issue with the army, as well. Since the reign of Marcus Aurelius, the army had grown dramatically, requiring increasingly large sums for maintenance. Army pay had been increased under Caracalla; troop bonuses for successful combat were common. No emperor wanted to incur the wrath of his soldiers by cutting back on either of these.

Economic Changes
A reasonable explanation, at least in part, for the empire's demise lies in economics, specifically, in the handling of the state finances. An endless torrent of gold and silver coins flowed out across the Roman borders. Gold and silver had increased in value in the third century, perhaps because of a shortage of the precious metals. It was tempting to hoard the precious metal, to reduce the proportion of gold, silver, and copper in the coins. The emperors after Marcus Aurelius and Commodus did so,

time and again. As the coins decreased in actual value, prices increased; less merchandise could be bought with the same coins. As a result, inflation and poverty increased alarmingly.

At the same time, the cost of running the government (including the military) had greatly increased. The state was unable to collect enough money through taxes to cover its ever-increasing expenditure. In response, the emperors levied the highest taxes in history.

The resultant lack of financial security dealt trade a heavy blow. Provinces had to rely on their own resources as the empire's economy began to disintegrate. The crisis hit the cities first, as artisans lost a large part of their market. Money was increasingly less important, as coinage grew increasingly worthless. Barter became popular, since money could not be trusted. As the tax burden burgeoned, a significant share of taxes was paid in kind. The urban rich were hit badly. It was from this group that honorary officials were chosen to act

The city of Trier
(Augusta Treverorum)
in Germany
was founded by the Emperor
Augustus and often
served as the imperial
residence. The Porta Nigra
(Black Gate) is one
of many Roman monuments
still to be found
in the city.

The servant of a large landowner,
pouring wine.
On the right of the relief,
we can see part of a
richly covered table.

as tax collectors. They had to personally guarantee the collection of taxes, which made them ruthless. Those who could fled the city for country homes and rural isolation. Remaining members of the elite were then hit even harder.

Less and less money was available for enhancing urban life with buildings and public celebrations. Yet walls often had to be built to protect the provincial cities against bands of plunderers, both barbarian and Roman army. Many cities, particularly in the western part of the em-pire, grew impoverished.

Epidemics were yet another factor in this general decline. Regularly wreaking havoc in the population, disease reduced available manpower below the level needed for routine maintenance of aqueducts, roads, and arable farmland. The number of slaves also declined, as the days of profitable wars, which brought tens of thousands of prisoners to the slave market, were over.

Landowners turned to different ways of farming. Instead of groups of slaves to work an entire estate, they used farming families who would lease part of it. These tenant farmers surrendered a fixed share of their income to the landowner. While it gave him lower profits than before, it did guarantee regular income, important in a time when sales to the cities of wine, oil, and other estate products were under serious threat.

The arrangement was also beneficial to the tenant farmers (or *coloni*, as they were called), providing some measure of protection in unsettled times. Occasionally, a small landowning farmer would even offer his acreage to a wealthy landowner in return for a contract as tenant farmer. Some landowners freed their slaves, making them into tenant farmers. The system became increasingly widespread in the second and

The two sides of a Roman coin, with the image of the Emperor Diocletian, who ruled from AD 285 to 305

Because the traditional provinces had outgrown the administrative machinery and the governors had attracted too much power to themselves, Diocletian redivided the empire. He created more than a hundred new provinces, grouped into 14 dioceses. These, in turn, were grouped into four prefectures (districts governed by a prefect), whose chief administrators were in close contact with the emperor. This division is still reflected today in the boundaries of many dioceses of the Roman Catholic Church.

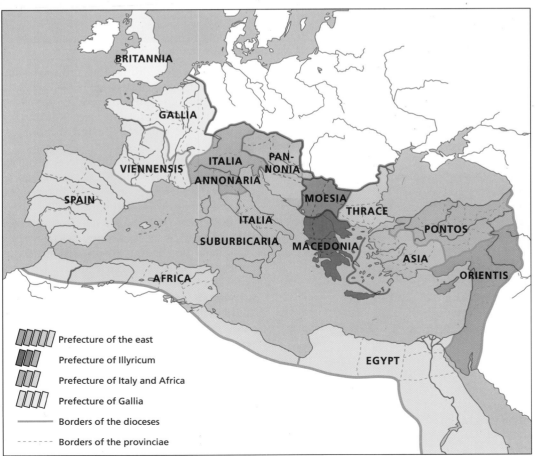

BRITANNIA
GALLIA
VIENNENSIS
SPAIN
ITALIA ANNONARIA
PAN-NONIA
ITALIA SUBURBICARIA
MACEDONIA
MOESIA
THRACE
PONTOS
ASIA
ORIENTIS
AFRICA
EGYPT

Prefecture of the east

Prefecture of Illyricum

Prefecture of Italy and Africa

Prefecture of Gallia

Borders of the dioceses

Borders of the provinciae

third centuries, with landowners attempting to tie their coloni to them. Eventually, the emperors would force successive generations of tenant farmers to stay on the estates, making them little better than slaves.

Economic problems varied throughout the empire. The Italian peninsula, the western provinces, and those along the Danube suffered more than those in North Africa and the east. Understanding of the economic process was limited. The economy of the Roman Empire had always been quite fragile, with the great mass of the population too poor to buy much. Now with the onset of civil unrest and increasing inflation, trade and industry, always focused on a limited circle of richer customers, were especially threatened.

The Illyrian Continuation
In AD 275, the Senate, for the first time in a while and at the request of the army, chose the successor to Aurelian, the old senator Tacitus. He resigned after less than a year, to be followed by the Illyrian general Probus.

After successful defense in AD 275–77 against Gallic invasion, Probus turned to economic reform. He used the army for public works, brought in foreigners to settle the provinces, and encouraged cultivation of abandoned farms. These ideas may have provoked his assassination at the hands of soldiers in 282.

Carus replaced him as emperor, sharing power with his sons Numerian and Carinus. The first two died in military campaign in Persia.

The Tetrarchy: Diocletian
In AD 284, another Illyrian, Diocles, seized power. A simple farmer's son, he had risen to general in the army of his murdered predecessor, Numerian. He was so popular with the soldiers that they made him emperor instead of Numerian's assassin, whom Diocles had executed. Changing his name to Diocletian, the new emperor subsequently defeated and killed Carinus.

Diocletian's power was precarious. Persians threatened in the east and Germans in the north. Gaul was perilous because of the *bacaudae*, armies of escaped coloni (tenant farmers reneging on their obligations) and unsettled farmers ruined by war and exploitation. Diocletian sent experienced commanders to reestablish Roman authority. Aware that victorious generals had often attempted to seize power in the past, he created the Rule of the Four Emperors to coopt those he sent. It allowed his successful commanders (all prestigious Illyrians

related to him by marriage or adoption) to join his rule. Diocletian was the sole statesman.

What he established was a new form of government, the four-way sharing of imperial power called the tetrarchy. A two-level collegium evolved, comprising the primary rank of Augustus and the secondary, Caesar. Major decision-making power rested with the two Augusti, Diocletian himself and General Maximian, who was promoted first to Colleague of the Emperor, in AD 285, and a year later to Augustus. (In fact, most important decisions were still made by Diocletian.) In 293, Diocletian and

In AD 68, Diocletian appointed a second augustus (ruler) to rule the western part of the Roman Empire. Maximian was appointed, seen here with Diocletian. See also page 831 for the two vice-emperors.

Detail of the Emperor Constantine's Arch, showing the triumphal procession of a Roman general. Enemy prisoners were usually included in such processions.

Maximian continued to hold the title of Augustus. Two other generals, Galerius and Constantius, were given executive power and the title Caesar.

Each emperor was handed a section of the Roman Empire to control, but no formal territorial division was made. Diocletian had the eastern part of the empire, Thrace, Egypt, and Asia; Maximian had the Italian peninsula and Africa; Galerius ruled the Danubian provinces; and Constantius had the western provinces of Gaul, the Iberian peninsula, and Britain. Each emperor had his own capital city. (Diocletian was in Nicomedia, the others in Milan, Trier, and Sirmium.) None of them lived in Rome. Diocletian, in providing threatened areas their own imperial protectors, had found a method of stabilizing government. By dividing power, he minimized the risk of usurpation. He retained overall supervision of the empire and the authority both to legislate and to appoint consuls.

The tetrarchy was transitory, but some of Diocletian's other reforms effected more permanent change. His actions undermined the dominance of Rome and the favored political and economic position of the Italian peninsula. He increased the number of provinces, giving them additional power. He grouped the new provinces into regions called dioceses under the administrative authority of officials called vicars. Provincial armies were increased in size, particularly in the border areas. Landowners were required to contribute either recruits or money to the army. Diocletian established, in addition, a tactical army and a special unit under his direct control. He put the command of all troops under professional soldiers and separated it from civilian authority.

The system of tetrarchy effectively quadrupled the government. Diocletian improved administrative efficiency in the provinces, especially tax collection, and usually appointed equestrian praesides (guardians or superintendents) rather than senators to govern them. They had no military importance, although they were required to be enrolled in the militia. They were responsible for all aspects of civilian administration, including police and legal matters and, above all, taxation. As responsibilities increased, so did the number of officials needed to carry them out. Such work became a recognized career. Diocletian, in effect, had created an imperial civil service.

The changes Diocletian implemented involved enormous increase in the costs of running the state. The huge expense had to be paid for by the public via increased taxes. Diocletian organized the empire as a coercive state, demanding universal cooperation in its maintenance. Anyone practicing an important profession was compelled to continue it for the rest of his life. Sons were to follow in their fathers' footsteps. The coloni, once tenant farmers with a right to some mobility, were tied to their land. He instituted price controls on food and other necessities and established maximum wages for workers. His efforts reduced the raging inflation he had inherited. Had he saved the empire? It continued to exist, but for many of its inhabitants, freedom was severely limited.

Deification

Diocletian considered himself responsible to no one, not even the other members of the tetrarchy. Receiving his present authority from the gods, he felt, he was sure he would take his place among them after his death. He wanted, in effect, to be considered a god while still alive. He invoked Roman religious tradition for support in these matters. Linking himself with Jupiter, he demanded to be known as Jovius. Maximian, his co-Augustus, was

Roman mosaic
from the fourth century AD:
two individuals
from the provinces,
protecting themselves
behind a shield

Ruins of the thermae
(baths) at Trier, Germany,
built by the Romans
at the end of
the third century

known as Herculius, son of Hercules. The
emperor's person and surroundings were
considered holy. It was not permitted to
approach him in normal fashion. He wore
costly garments, set with precious gems.
Incense and candles were lit in his
presence. The title of princeps was now
replaced entirely by dominus or lord.
Roman citizens had, indeed, become the
slaves or subjects of this lord.

Diocletian required unity and absolute
obedience, which put him in conflict with
the Christians like his predecessor Decius.
Disturbed by the increasing number of
Christians in the army and in his court, he
sought to put an end to the church once and
for all. The final, and fiercest, persecutions
began in AD 303, primarily in the east
where Diocletian himself reigned with
Galerius. By this time the new faith was too
widespread to be destroyed, however many
martyrs died. Persecutions had diminished
by the time Diocletian abdicated in 305.
Several years later they would stop entirely.

Imperial Succession
Succession to the emperorship was another
issue. State law in the Principate had never
recognized a right of succession. Diocletian

advocated divine monarchy. He passed
legislation completely removing the Senate's power, rendering it little more than an
honorary city council for Rome.

On May 1, AD 305, Diocletian and
Maximian each abdicated as Augustus to
make way for Galerius and Constantius, the
Caesars under them. Two new Caesars
were appointed, despite the fact that
Maximian and Constantius each had sons.
(Diocletian's dominant personality held the
four emperors together until he chose to
abdicate. Why he did so is unclear. He may
have agreed long before that he and
Maximian would only rule for twenty
years. In any case, he had to force
Maximian to follow.)

The Second Tetrarchy
By AD 306, it became clear that the system
of tetrarchy was not working. The people
and the army preferred the old hereditary
principle. The two new Caesars of the second tetrarchy were Severus and Maximinus
Daia. When the new Augustus Constantius
died at Eburacum, he was not succeeded by
his designated Caesar. The armies of Gaul
and Britain, disregarding the rules of the
tetrarchy, appointed Constantius's son Con-

stantine as Augustus. Maxentius, one of Maximian's sons, promptly got himself proclaimed in Rome, ignoring the Caesar Severus.

In AD 307–308, seven men claimed themselves Augustus: Maximian, Galerius, Constantine, Maxentius, Maximinus Daia, Licinius (who had been declared Augustus against Constantine by Galerius), and Domitius Alexander (in Africa). From his palace at Aspalathos in Dalmatia, Diocletian could only watch while his imaginative system brought discord and civil war for years.

Constantine

Natural death and murder by intrigue led to a standoff by AD 311: Constantine and Maxentius in the west, Licinius and Maximus Daia in the east.

Constantine, the strongest general, entered Italy to defeat Maxentius (who drowned while escaping) near Rome at the Battle of the Milvian Bridge. The campaign is most noted for its effect on the victorious emperor. During it, Constantine claimed he had a vision of the cross. Afterward, he declared himself a Christian. Joining military forces with Licinius (who sealed the arrangement later by marrying Constantine's sister), he won over the eastern Christians with the AD 313 Edict of Milan guaranteeing them tolerance. Maximinus Daia, ill and defeated by Licinius, died the same year.

Constantine emerged from the contest as victor, initially in the west in AD 312. In 316, he parted with Licinius for the first time, taking a couple of dioceses (Pannonia and Moesia) from him, only to then arrange a ten-year truce. That was the same year that Diocletian died. Both emperors then abandoned his concept of tetrarchy for good, asserting the principle of heredity on behalf of their assorted infant sons.

One of the major issues between the two was Christianity. Licinius favored persecution; Constantine converted, an event of extraordinary long-term significance throughout the empire and beyond. In AD 324, tensions flared again at Hadrianople. Constantine defeated Licinius, then forced his surrender and his execution with his son in Asia Minor.

This left Constantine the uncontested ruler of the Roman empire. He had made Christianity its official religion. In AD 324, he established the new administrative headquarters of the empire on the site of Byzantium, calling it Nova Roma (or New Rome, dedicated in 330). Strategically located in terms of the Danube and the Euphrates, as well as commercially well positioned on major trading routes, this would become the major city of Constantinople (present-day Istanbul). Constantine made it also the urban center of Christianity.

The emperor continued many of the reforms instituted by Diocletian. He main-

tained the separate forces of the *limitanei* (border guards) and the *comitatenses* (tactical troops and imperial guard). Continuing the practice of independent military and civil careers, he modified the ranking system within the government administration to provide recognition and enhanced prestige to worthy individuals. He expanded the territorial jurisdiction and authority of the praetorian prefects, setting the dio-

The Emperor Diocletian appointed Constantine and Galerius (here pictured together) as Caesars. Their function, a mixture of governor and king, was to help the two emperors (Diocletian and Maximian) maintain Roman rule.

831

The mausoleum erected in memory of the Emperor Constantine the Great (AD 306–337) and his family. Constantine granted equal rights in 313 to Christians and non-Christians in the Edict of Milan and was baptized on his deathbed.

cesan vicars under them. He established four great prefectures: the east, the Italian peninsula, Gaul, and Illyricum.

Constantine the Christian ransacked the traditional temples and the treasury of Licinius and used the spoils to benefit the state. He had two new coins minted, the silver miliarensis and the gold solidus, as solid as its name. (It would become the basic currency of the Byzantine Empire.)

In AD 337, he relinquished his power to his three sons, each designated Caesar. (A fourth son, Crispus, had been executed in 326.) They divided the empire: Constantine II in the west, Constantius in the east, and Constans, in Africa, the Italian peninsula, and Illyricum. (Together they constituted the second Flavian dynasty, through Constantine's father Flavius Constantius.) Constantine died on May 22, 337, having been baptized on his deathbed.

Fourth-century Emperors

Rivalry and death followed. Constans killed Constantine II for trying to seize his territory in AD 340, only to be killed himself a decade later by the usurper Magnentius. The remaining brother, Constantius, reunited the empire as Augustus in 353, eventually naming his nephews as Caesars.

Both were poor choices. One (Gallus) proved incompetent and had to be eliminated; the other (Julian) so competent as to be declared Augustus himself in 361. War was avoided when Constantius died in November that year.

Julian (AD 361–363)

Julian the Apostate (so named for his renunciation of Christianity) reinstated the pagan religion undone by Constantine. In an attempt to restore national confidence, he undertook a military campaign against the Persians that cost him his life.

Jovian (AD 363–364)
Julian's successor, Jovian, put in place by the army, was a moderate Christian with a policy of tolerance. He negotiated a peace with Shapur I in Persia that cost Rome considerable territory, including Nisibis and Armenia. He died by accident in 364.

Separation of the Empire: AD 364
Valentinian, another moderate Christian, was made emperor in the west by the army, but forced to share power in the east with his inept brother Valens. This division was a reflection of the one within the army itself. With the help of his general Theodosius the Elder, Valentinian successfully fought a number of border campaigns in Gaul and Pannonia and revolts in Africa and Britain. On the domestic front, while he terrorized the senatorial elite, he took steps to protect the poor, to maintain a strong administrative and tax collection system, and to encourage religious tolerance.

Valens, fanatically Christian, was reinforced in his convictions by the praetorian

Partial views of the inside and the dome of the Pantheon, a temple devoted to all the Roman gods. Built in Rome by the Emperor Hadrian, it has been maintained in good condition since 609, when it first came into use as a Christian church, the Santa Maria Rotunda.

The Arch of Constantine the Great in Rome. Its reliefs were taken from existing monuments.

prefect Modestus and began pagan persecutions. He faced down the usurpation of the pagan Procopius in 356-366 with the aid of his loyal army but was killed in battle at Hadrianople in 378.

Gratian

Valentinian died abruptly in AD 375. His son Gratian took over the west, sharing nominal eastern power at the insistence of the Pannonian army with his four-year-old brother Valentinian II.

Theodosius the Great (AD 379–395)

In AD 379, Gratian declared Theodosius emperor in the east. The son of Valentinian's famous general (who had just been executed, a victim of Pannonian jealousy), Theodosius was selected because of his own military ability and his religious orthodoxy. He would use the first to implement the second, establishing the bishop of Nicaea in Constantinople as equal to the bishop of Rome. Theologically, this split the empire east and west in 381.

The action annoyed both western Arian Christians (who had been deposed in Constantinople) and powerful pagans in the army of Gaul and Britain. It declared its leader Maximus emperor in AD 383. Maximus entered Gaul, killed Gratian, was first recognized by Theodosius, and then killed by him after invading the Italian peninsula in 388.

Theodosius now had both east and west. (The third Augustus, Valentinian II, never significant, died mysteriously in AD 392.) Until his death in 395, Theodosius ruled an undivided empire.

His two sons again divided it, sharing their rule. This was the final division of the empire into a western half, which was to collapse in the fifth century, and an eastern, which was to survive another thousand years.

Constantius, the son of Constantine, inherited the eastern Roman empire after his father's death. In AD 355 he appointed his cousins Galus and Julian as Caesars. When Julian was proclaimed emperor by the army, Constantius marched against him, but fell ill and died before the battle.

Marble relief with a portrait of the Emperor Antoninus Pius at Eleusis, Greece

Allies and Enemies

At the Edge of the Roman Empire

The seafarers of ancient Rome rarely ventured beyond the "Pillars of Hercules" (today's Straits of Gibraltar) guarding the western entrance of the Mediterranean. Most Romans thought the ocean beyond it was bounded by the edge of the world. To the peasant people who first established the minor settlement that would be Rome on the Italian peninsula in the eighth century BC, the edge of the world was very close.

Eventually, the Mediterranean Sea became a Roman lake, stolen from Carthage in the second century BC. By the late fourth century AD, the Romans knew all its shores and beyond. They had taken the peninsula and every island in the sea, and spread an empire and a way of life in every direction. Their dominion ran from Europe, including Britain, through the Near and Middle East, to Egypt and north Africa. Now they touched many seas: nearby, the Adriatic and the Aegean; the Atlantic and the North; the Black, the Caspian, and the Red.

Through centuries of conquest, they touched many peoples, as well, leaving an impression that has not yet disappeared. Certain of their own identity, confident in their gods, they created a civilization that, for the most part, attempted to assimilate those it conquered, leaving an indelible stamp on administration, law, language, and culture. In both the republic and the empire, the Romans placed great emphasis on the toleration of intercultural difference. It enabled the inculcation of their own culture wherever they went and is one of the reasons for their long-term success. The policy began early.

Romans in battle with "barbarians," as shown on a sarcophagus from the times of Marcus Aurelius

The Italian Peninsula

During the seventh century, the Latin people of Rome clung to that early culture even under Etruscan hegemony. After the Etruscans seized direct power (about 550 BC) and literally built Rome into a major city, surrounding it with a stone wall, their influence on the Romans was far greater. The Etruscans gave them an alphabet, learned from the Greeks, and some ac-

quaintance with Hellenistic thought. But the temples they erected were to the Roman gods and the structure of the Latin language, as well as Roman social and political practices, remained unique.

In the fifth century BC, Rome had problems with incursions by the mountain people of the central Apennines, the Sabines and the Aequi and, from the south, by the Hernici and the Volsci of the Lepini mountains. There was extended interurban conflict, as well, with the Etruscan city of Veii, finally captured in 395 BC.

Five years later came the *dies religiosus* (the accursed day), the occupation of Rome by Gallic invaders. (They had been periodically making their presence known on the Italian peninsula since the sixth century BC.) The nearby Etruscan city of Caere took in the sacred objects salvaged from Rome, creating a bond between the cities. The result, after the invaders left, was the precedent-setting granting of Roman citizenship (without suffrage) to Caerites.

Rome moved to take over the towns of Latium, assigning varied kinds of status as it did. Tusculum and Lavinium were made *municipia* (municipal towns in which *civitas sine suffragio*, citizenship without the right to vote, was assigned), for example, while Tibur and Praeneste were made *civitates foederatae* (allied cities). Such allies were not subjugated by the Romans but the alliances were never quite of complete equality. Tolerance was the norm, yet despite the fact that the foederati (the people of the allied cities) were allowed to maintain their own social institutions, religions, and systems of government, unless these posed a direct threat to Rome, the Romans retained the upper hand.

By the Third Samnite War (the Samnite Wars ran on intermittently from 343 BC to 265 BC), the Etruscans, the Gauls, and the Samnites (skilled mountain warriors) had united against the encroaching Roman presence in the northern half of the peninsula—to no avail. Etruria fell to Rome at last, the Gallic incursions were halted, and Rome's influence spread south through the Lucanian and Apulian peoples.

Pyrrhus, Greek king of Epirus, tried and failed to unite the Hellenic cities of southern Italy in opposition. With the defeat of the predominant city Tarentum (accorded allied status in 271 BC), Roman hegemony on the peninsula was complete. The principles of conquest, the honorable treatment of the defeated, had been established. As Roman colonists moved in, the

techniques of colonization and the obligations of the new colonies to Rome were likewise established.

In 306 BC, Rome and Carthage, still maintaining good relations, renewed what was to be their last agreement to avoid intervention in each other's political domain: Carthage was to stay out of Italy and Rome to stay away from Sicily. Rome had become a commercial giant, influential even in the Hellenic world, but was not yet a naval power. Carthage controlled the Mediterranean.

The Public Provinces
Sicily: 241 BC
Corsica and Sardinia: 238 BC
In 264 BC, Rome invaded Sicily, interfering in its internal affairs in violation of the 306 BC agreement. Rome did so at the request of mercenaries who had seized the island's major city, Messana, and were afraid they would lose it to Carthage. Rome had no interest in having that dominant navy harbored so close to the tip of its own peninsular boot. The result was the first Punic War. By 241 BC, Rome itself had become a significant naval power and Sicily had become its first province. It added the islands of Corsica and Sardinia as the second, always governed jointly, in 238 BC.

By the end of the Third Punic War in 133 BC, Rome had conquered Cisalpine Gaul, capping the Italian peninsula, most of Spain, the tip of north Africa that had belonged to Carthage, the northern shore of the Adriatic, and (as a result of the three Macedonian Wars) most of the Hellenistic world. Rome's policies had grown increas-

Roman citizens from the Rhine provinces paying taxes to Roman deputies; marble relief from the third century AD

ingly harsh as it conquered and developed seven provinces.

Nearer and Farther Spain : 197 BC

Nearer and Farther Spain, originally declared as two separate provinces as part of the Punic campaigns in 197 BC, were to present far greater problems than the islands of the Mediterranean. Resistance was always fierce in the mountains. The Roman policy of requiring whole communities of indigenous people to resettle in the plains was in its very essence so unpopular as to be unenforceable.

Both the Celtiberi of Nearer Spain and the Lusitani of Farther Spain fought unceasingly, even after the death of the noted resistance leader Viriathus in 139 BC. There were even related crises back in Rome. Wars were fought by armies and those armies had to be raised by levies on the general population. In 151 and 138 BC, Roman tribunes threw their own consuls into prison to stop them from issuing the levies. This was resolved in 134 BC by the consul Publius Cornelius Scipio Aemilianus who raised an army from private clients and thus avoided the levy. (He was familiar with the problems. The legal age requirement for consul had been lowered in 210 BC to allow him to be elected and sent to command in Spain.) He destroyed the Spanish stronghold of Numantia in 133 BC, slaughtering or enslaving its inhabitants.

Macedonia: 146 BC

Originally, the Roman Empire was a western phenomenon but after three Macedonian Wars (that ran from 215–168 BC), it came to dominate the east, as well. Rome's involvement began with its conquering of Macedonia's king, Philip V, an ally of Hannibal. His intent to rule the Aegean led to the second war and, again, defeat. Rome established a protectorate over Greece and then, allied with Greece, defeated the king of Syria to gain parts of Europe and Asia Minor. Philip's son Perseus necessitated the Third Macedonian War, ending in his capture in 168 BC.

Macedonia was subjugated and divided by Rome into four independent republics.

Ruins of a temple at the Roman port of Ostia

(Illyria was also divided into three parts, but first 150,000 of its male inhabitants were sold into slavery.) The province of Macedonia (including Illyria, Epirus, and Achaea) was established in 146 BC. That same year, the Achaean League staged a revolt in Greece which led to the plundering and total destruction of the city of Corinth by Rome.

Africa: 146 BC

In 146 BC, as well, Publius Cornelius Scipio Aemilianus Africanus Minor closed the Third Punic War with the capture and destruction of Carthage. This ended the Carthaginian empire. Its lands were made the Roman province of Africa.

Roman power never extended far into Africa. Like the Carthaginians before them, Romans were satisfied with the fertile regions on the northern coast of that continent. They organized occasional scouting expeditions into it, but the great Sahara Desert south of the coastal rim remained a terrifying barrier. Roman relations with the Berbers, tribal horsemen of great repute who lived in the deserts of what are present-day Morocco and Algeria, were almost always good. Their King Masinissa helped the Romans battle Hannibal of Carthage (the archenemy of both). The Romans greatly admired the Berbers and left the feudal rulers in Mauretania in peace.

Every large Roman city had an open-air theater where tragedies and comedies were performed. Shown are the remains of the Roman theater at Cyrene, a city in what is now Libya.

A succession crisis about 120 BC led to a brief war (112–105 BC), when the bastard king Jugurtha, supported by connections in Rome, sought to claim the shares of his two legitimate brothers in their divided kingdom.

Otherwise, Roman civilization developed in peace in the rich coastal areas. Numerous ruins of Roman cities and villas are still silent witnesses to that culture. Until the third century AD, when unrest spread here as elsewhere in the empire, problems arose only with a few desert nomads.

Asia (Pergamum): 133 BC

The kingdom of Pergamum remained an independent client kingdom until the death of its last king, Attalus III, in 133 BC. Having no heirs, he had bequeathed the region to Rome. It became the seventh Roman province and was named Asia.

Egypt

From 27 BC on, Roman provinces were of two types: those in the long-standing public category and the newer, more strategically important ones. Of the second category, Egypt was most important. Augustus took over the area from Cleopatra and, with it, all her problems. For centuries, Egypt had been competing with the Nubians, the black people inhabiting part of what is today's nation of Sudan. By his time, they had become formidable opponents. Their empire around the city of Meroë was reminiscent of the old Egypt of the pha-

Part of a statue of a Roman soldier found in Alexandria, Egypt. Only the torso, with Egyptian inscription, has been preserved.

Relief from Trajan's Column: the decapitation of captured barbarians by Roman soldiers

Integration on the Border: The Foederati

The tribes living on the borders of the Roman Empire were not part of its provincial division. The people were not usually subjugated by the Romans but, instead, treated as allies (or *foederati*). However, there was no such thing as equal alliance. Despite the fact that the foederati were allowed to maintain their own institutions, legal, and state systems, the Romans did retain the upper hand. In the third century AD, the empire was riddled with internal strife. Countless groups living on the borders grabbed the chance to invade. In the east, the Goths caused major destruction. In the west, the border was maintained with difficulty. There were even plunderers in normally quiet Africa.

In the third century AD, the empire was riddled with internal strife. Numerous tribes living on the borders saw the situation as ripe for exploitation and took the chance to invade the provinces. They were often defeated by the Roman armies but those victories were never conclusive. Provincial inhabitants were weary of the battles. The Romans decided to allow both foederati (designated allies) and invading groups to settle in the empire on the condition that they accept Roman authority. The decision allowed both immediate peace and the use of the new settlers as buffers against future attacks. The solution became an indispensable part of the Roman defense system. The extent to which Romanization of the settlers occurred is evident in the many Latin-based (or romance) languages spoken in much of Europe today.

Triumphal arch for the Emperor Septimius Severus at the Forum Romanum in Rome. The emperor had this arch erected in honor of his return after the Parthian campaign.

raohs. Their Queen Candace sent warrior bands on raids into southern Egypt. Since Roman grain supplies depended on Egyptian fields, Augustus sent an expeditionary army to defeat the Nubian Queen. Roman troops penetrated the area near Meroë where they established the southernmost outpost of the empire to maintain control. In spite of this, Roman influence other than on the coast remained minor.

Europe

The first Roman Emperor Augustus advised his successor not to extend the boundaries of the empire further, especially in Europe. His successor Tiberius and the great majority of emperors after him kept that advice, regarding the Rhine and the Danube Rivers as natural boundaries on the European continent. It was exceptional for Romans to seek conquest across them. It was not in the interest of the emperors themselves to allow their generals (as both

their subordinates and their potential rivals) to gain glory by such conquest, nor did they want the expense of military campaigning.

Romans had little knowledge of the world outside their empire, particularly with regard to the peoples of northern Europe. What they did know did not make them eager to bring these regions into the empire. A few Roman intellectuals, notably the historian Tacitus, thought highly of the Germans. They thought they could recognize some of the old Roman virtues in the Germans: simplicity, a life on the land, personal fidelity, and great bravery. The Germans, according to Tacitus, were as yet unspoiled by the pleasures of the civilized world.

In reality, German life was far from ideal. Most groups lived in great poverty, constantly involved in small wars. Led by a kind of aristocracy, only in times of emergency did they elect a leader or a king, who was "lifted on the shield" in a meeting of free men. The power of these leaders depended largely on their success. Those who led their people into the rich regions of the Romans seem to have acquired enormous prestige, eventually making their kingships hereditary.

In the far west province of Britain and north of Hadrian's Wall lived a group of people as wild as the Germans. The Romans called them Picts but knew little about them. The Celts south of the wall had accepted the authority of the Roman governor, who, although responsible for their security, was never quite able to prevent the Picts from raiding across the wall.

The Parthians

On its eastern border, the Roman Empire hardly ever extended beyond the River Euphrates. The Parthians ruled on the other side. They lived for centuries in what is today northeastern Iran, divided into small, strictly patriarchal groups. They gave the Persian kings and the first Seleucians little trouble until after the Bactrian rebellion against the Seleucian king in 250 BC. Then Parthian King Arsaces succeeded in gaining independence from Rome and extending his territory southwest. Over the next two hundred years, the Parthians used the weakening of the Seleucian Empire to

Female slaves helping their mistress get dressed. This marble relief was found in the Roman city of Noviomagus (present-day Neumagen, Germany).

increase their own power, until they controlled all of ancient Persia and Mesopotamia. They established the city of Ktesifon, on the River Tigris, as their new capital. By 64 BC, once Pompey had created the province of Syria out of the remainder of the Seleucian Empire, the Parthians became Rome's neighbors and rivals on the Euphrates — remaining so for three hundred years.

Bronze lion from the Parthian Empire, made in the first century AD

Relief from Dalmatia, representing a hunting scene. The figure on the left throws a spear, while the man on the extreme right prepares a beheaded animal for a meal.

Emperor Trajan mounted a huge expedition and conquered the whole of Mesopotamia in AD 114–117, destroying the Parthian capital. His death prevented a solid defense of the conquered areas. His successor Emperor Hadrian gave up Mesopotamia again and made peace. The Parthians never really got over the blow that Trajan had dealt them, due largely to the weak political organization of their empire. In spirit, they had always remained a nomadic people, not permanently rooted in the ancient lands of Mesopotamia and Persia.

In the second century AD, the Parthians suffered another heavy defeat at the hands of the Romans. By 200, Septimius Severus annexed the north of Mesopotamia to the Roman Empire. A revolution in 226 replaced the Parthian aristocracy with a new dynasty of rulers, the Persian Sasanides. Intent on restoring the old Persian Empire, they continued the centuries-old war against Rome with renewed energy, but the many wars that followed would lead only to a weakening of both empires.

Arabia

For centuries, cargo ships plied the Red Sea, bound for the mysterious merchant cities of southern Arabia. Their inhabitants owed their wealth to the supply of Indian spices and their own desert products like incense. They traded with merchants from Egypt and Syria, who called the area around the city of Aden "Happy Arabia" because of its extensive irrigation works and resultant prosperity.

In the second century BC, seafarers from Egypt discovered the monsoon wind. Blowing constantly across the Indian ocean from west to east, it made direct voyages to India possible. The inhabitants of southern Arabia lost their function as the go-betweens of Indian products.

At the same time that he mounted the expedition against the Nubians, Augustus sent an army to Arabia. The campaign was a terrible failure. Even before they reached Aden, the survivors had to turn back empty-handed.

Southern Arabia would retain importance only as a supplier of incense, transported north by caravan via the old trading center of Mecca. As once-happy Arabia declined, its irrigation works fell into disuse. By the Middle Ages, the area was little different from the rest of the barren peninsula.

A heavily loaded ship being pulled by slaves, with the master at the helm. Note the baskets and jars above the ship, that were used for the transport of goods.

India

Beyond the Parthian Empire lay India, in contact since Alexander the Great with the Greeks and, later, the Greco-Roman world. Alexander left the Indus region with his army in 325 BC, his conquests there soon undone by the Indian Prince Chandragupta, who, in turn, established the first great empire in India, with Pataliputra on the River Ganges as its capital. In 305 BC, Chandragupta concluded a treaty with Seleucus, Alexander's successor in Asia, gaining authority over the whole Indus valley and its western approaches in exchange for five hundred war elephants. The Hellenistic kings of Syria and Egypt sent ambassadors to him. One of these, Megasthenes, reported about 290 BC on the situation in Chandragupta's empire. Although he repeats some fanciful stories from hearsay, he credibly describes everything he observed, especially the royal roads, the capital Pataliputra (near present-day Benares), and the caste system of Indian society. Chandragupta kept court in a large golden palace where he lived with his harem and a bodyguard of women soldiers, in all probability Greek.

Megathenes hints at the existence of Buddhism which was gaining increasing popularity during this time. Chandragupta's grandson, King Asoka, converted to this new religion about the middle of the third century BC, preaching to his subjects and sending missionaries to areas of India which had not yet taken to it. (It is said that he also sent missionaries to the Greek kingdoms but Greek sources do not mention visitors from India.) With Asoka's support, Buddhism spread widely in the third century, south to present-day Sri Lanka and north to central Asia. With the rise of the Parthian Empire, contact between India and the west grew more difficult. This changed when the monsoon winds were discovered in the second century BC, enabling trade via the Red Sea and the Arabian Sea. India offered pepper, cinnamon, nutmeg, and mace; textiles; gemstones; pearls; ivory; and exotic animals in exchange for Alexandrian glass, bronze kitchenware, and minted gold and silver coins. Trade between Egypt and India expanded enormously after Egypt was incorporated into the Roman Empire. Many Roman coins have been found on the coasts of India, proving that trading contacts were frequent. Some seafarers ventured even further to the east, to the coasts of Indo-China.

Trade with India always dealt in luxuries, paid for in gold or silver. As long as the Roman Empire remained strong and the upper class of society rich, this trade continued. With the decline of the Roman Empire during the fourth and fifth centuries AD, it gradually disappeared.

China

Romans evidently knew no more about

Ruins of the temple built during Emperor Trajan's reign at Pergamum, Turkey

China than that it lay far to the east and produced silk. In the second century BC, an emperor of the Han dynasty sent an expedition to the west to explore and find allies against threatening nomads. An emissary returned after years to report the existence of rich cities and fertile lands around the region of present-day Uzbekistan. Caravan routes led from there to the west, to Iran, Mesopotamia, and Syria. The Chinese court sent more expeditions, loaded with silk, which had always found eager buyers among foreigners. Any alliance faded in the face of trade. Steady processions of merchants with their pack animals now moved from China to the Stone Tower at the foot of the Pamir Mountains. There, the goods were taken over by Iranian and Syrian traders and moved further west. In exchange, Greek industrial products, and especially gold and silver, were taken east. This is the famous Silk Route. Created toward the end of the second century BC, it would, with many interruptions, remain the only link between China and the west until the Middle Ages.

The Chinese themselves never penetrated the countries belonging to Greco-Roman civilization, but during the reign of Domitian, an exploratory mission did reach Mesopotamia. It reported to the Chinese emperor a rich empire to the west of Mesopotamia, with Antioch at its center. This was the Roman province of Syria, thought to be a separate state by the Chinese.

Roman subjects, on the other hand, did reach China. In the first century AD, a ship's captain from Alexandria probably reached a port in southern China; in the second and third centuries, small groups of Syrian merchants reached the residence of the Chinese emperors, pretending to be ambassadors of the Roman emperor to enhance their prestige. Apart from such exploratory missions, contact was limited. The empires were simply too far apart. By the fourth century AD, Rome appears to have forgotten again the little it knew about the land of silk.

Roman gravestone
with inscription, found in
the Spanish province
of Tarragona

In antiquity there were already many trading contacts between the largest countries. This small map shows a survey of the trading routes in the second century AD.

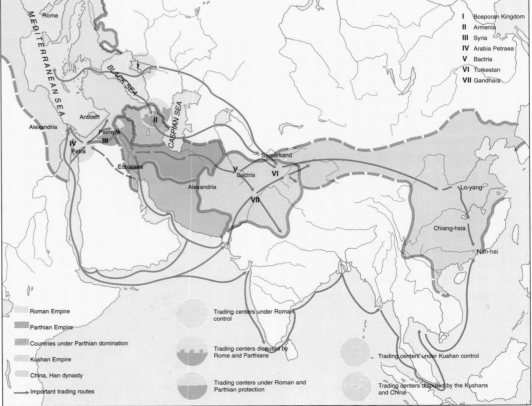

I Bosporan Kingdom
II Armenia
III Syria
IV Arabia Petraea
V Bactria
VI Turkestan
VII Gandhara

Roman Empire
Parthian Empire
Countries under Parthian domination
Kushan Empire
China, Han dynasty
Important trading routes

Trading centers under Roman control
Trading centers disputed by Rome and Parthians
Trading centers under Roman and Parthian protection
Trading centers under Kushan control
Trading centers disputed by the Kushans and China

846

TIME LINE

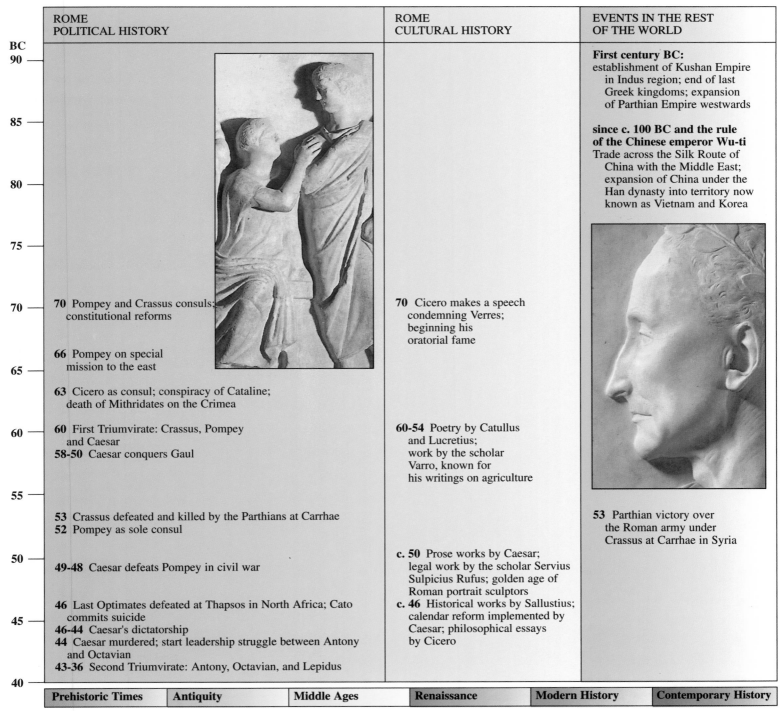

ROME POLITICAL HISTORY	ROME CULTURAL HISTORY	EVENTS IN THE REST OF THE WORLD
		First century BC: establishment of Kushan Empire in Indus region; end of last Greek kingdoms; expansion of Parthian Empire westwards
		since c. 100 BC and the rule of the Chinese emperor Wu-ti Trade across the Silk Route of China with the Middle East; expansion of China under the Han dynasty into territory now known as Vietnam and Korea
70 Pompey and Crassus consuls; constitutional reforms	**70** Cicero makes a speech condemning Verres; beginning his oratorial fame	
66 Pompey on special mission to the east		
63 Cicero as consul; conspiracy of Cataline; death of Mithridates on the Crimea		
60 First Triumvirate: Crassus, Pompey and Caesar **58-50** Caesar conquers Gaul	**60-54** Poetry by Catullus and Lucretius; work by the scholar Varro, known for his writings on agriculture	
53 Crassus defeated and killed by the Parthians at Carrhae **52** Pompey as sole consul		**53** Parthian victory over the Roman army under Crassus at Carrhae in Syria
49-48 Caesar defeats Pompey in civil war	**c. 50** Prose works by Caesar; legal work by the scholar Servius Sulpicius Rufus; golden age of Roman portrait sculptors	
46 Last Optimates defeated at Thapsos in North Africa; Cato commits suicide **46-44** Caesar's dictatorship **44** Caesar murdered; start leadership struggle between Antony and Octavian **43-36** Second Triumvirate: Antony, Octavian, and Lepidus	**c. 46** Historical works by Sallustius; calendar reform implemented by Caesar; philosophical essays by Cicero	

BC
90
85
80
75
70
65
60
55
50
45
40

| Prehistoric Times | Antiquity | Middle Ages | Renaissance | Modern History | Contemporary History |

	ROME POLITICAL HISTORY	ROME CULTURAL HISTORY	EVENTS IN THE REST OF THE WORLD
40		**40** Virgil's *Eclogues*	
35			
30	**31** Battle of Actium: Antony and Cleopatra's fleet defeated **30** Octavian annexes Egypt; suicide of Antony and Cleopatra **27** Octavian given new name, Augustus; start of the Principate	**29** Virgil begins *The Aeneid* **28** Foundation of library in the Temple of Apollo on the Palatine in Rome; love verses by Propertius; building of the original Pantheon in Rome; Livy begins *History of Rome from the Foundation of the City*	
25			
20			
15		**17** Celebration of the century festival in Rome: *Carmen saeculare* by Horace **14** Textbook by Vitruvius on architecture; work by geographer Strabo	
10	**9** Three legions destroyed in Germany; Rhine and Danube become borders of the empire	**9** Altar of Peace consecrated in Rome	**9** End of the western Han dynasty; revolution under Wang Mang, attempting to impose radical reforms
5			
AD 0		**3** Forum of Augustus, with the Temple of Mars the Avenger, consecrated in Rome	
5			**1st century AD**: growth of Kushan Empire in northwest India; expansion of Buddhism from central Asia into China; Greek-Buddhist art in Ganddhara style in area of India, Pakistan and Afghanistan; sea trade between India and the Roman Empire; trade along the Silk Route between China and the Near East
10		**8** Poet Ovid exiled to the Black Sea coast	
15	**14** Augustus dies; Tiberius succeeds him **14-37** Tiberius	**14** Mausoleum of Augustus in Rome	
20			
25	**26** Tiberius leaves for Capri; the Praetorian Prefect Sejanus increases his influence		**25** Restoration of (now eastern) Han dynasty; paper invented in China
30		**28** Villa of Tiberius on Capri	

Prehistoric Times	Antiquity	Middle Ages	Renaissance	Modern History	Contemporary History

ROME POLITICAL HISTORY	ROME CULTURAL HISTORY	EVENTS IN THE REST OF THE WORLD
31 Sejanus executed		
37-41 Caligula	**37** Temple for Augustus completed in Rome; work by Jewish philosopher Filo	
41-54 Claudius	**40-50** Essays by Stoic philosopher Seneca; golden age of mural art (remains preserved at Pompeii)	
43 Start of the conquest of Britain		
48 Claudius marries Agrippina		
50 Claudius adopts Nero, son of Agrippina	**50-64** Essays by Christian Apostle Paul; encyclopedic work by scholar Pliny the Elder; poet Lucan in Rome; novel *Satyricon* by Petronius	
54 Agrippina poisons Claudius		
54-68 Nero		
59 Nero murders his mother, Agrippina		
64 Great Fire in Rome; persecution of the Christians	**64-68** Nero's Golden House in Rome	
68 Revolts in Gaul and Spain; Nero commits suicide		
68-69 Year of the Four Emperors (Galba, Otho, Vitellius and Vespasian) and civil war		
69-79 Vespasian		**c. 70** Chinese campaign progresses as far as Mesopotamia; vague accounts of Roman Empire in China
70 Fall of Jerusalem	**71** Triumphal arch of Titus in Rome; start of Colosseum construction	
79-81 Titus	**79** Temple of Vespasian in Rome; historical works by Jewish writer Flavius Josephus; poet Martial	
79 Eruption of Mt. Vesuvius; Pompeii and Herculaneum destroyed		
81-96 Domitian		
	c. 90 Satirical poems by Juvenal	
96 Domitian murdered; Senator Nerva becomes emperor		
96-98 Nerva		
98-117 Trajan		

Prehistoric Times	Antiquity	Middle Ages	Renaissance	Modern History	Contemporary History

ROME POLITICAL HISTORY	ROME CULTURAL HISTORY	EVENTS IN THE REST OF THE WORLD
		c. 100 Kanishka, king of the Kushans
102 Trajan's First Dacian war		
105-116 Second Dacian war; Dacia annexed as province		
	c. 110 Trajan's Forum in Rome, with basilica; Trajan's Column	
114-117 Trajan's war against the Parthians; conquest of Mesopotamia	**c. 115** Historical works by Tacitus; poems by Stoic philosopher Epictetus	
117 Death of Trajan; adoptive son Hadrian succeeds him	**c. 120** Hadrian's villa in Tivoli; biographies of the emperors by Suetonius; works by Greek scholar Plutarch	**c. 120** Further expansion of Buddhism; *Lotus Sutra,* most important Buddhist text, written
117-138 Hadrian		
132-135 Last major Jewish revolt in Judaea suppressed		
138 Death of Hadrian		
138-161 Antoninus Pius		**c. 140** Internal weakening of China; peasant's revolt led by Taoist League of the Yellow Turbans; astronomy and alchemy flourish in China
	c. 150 Rhetorical works by Fronto; astronomical and geographical works by Claudius Ptolemaeus (Ptolemy) in Egypt; Latin novel *Metamorphoses* by Apuleius	
161-180 Marcus Aurelius	**c. 160** *Institutes* by the lawyer Gaius; rebuilding of Athens by Herod Atticus; works by the physician Galen; satirical prose by the Greek Lucian	**c. 160** Revival of classical Hinduism in India
162-165 War against the Parthians; plague throughout the empire		**166** Syrian merchants at the court of the Chinese emperor

Prehistoric Times	Antiquity	Middle Ages	Renaissance	Modern History	Contemporary History

	ROME POLITICAL HISTORY	ROME CULTURAL HISTORY	EVENTS IN THE REST OF THE WORLD
170	**170-180** Campaigns of Marcus Aurelius on the Danube against Germans and Sarmations	**c. 170** Equestrian statue of Marcus Aurelius in Rome; description of Greece by Pausanias	
175			
180	**180** Death of Marcus Aurelius in a Danube army camp, his son Commodus succeeds him **180-192** Commodus		
185			
190		**190** Works by Christian writers Tertullian and Irenaeus	
195	**192** Commodus murdered; Senator Pertinax proclaimed emperor **193** Pertinax murdered by Praetorians; Didius Julianus made emperor in Rome; legions on the Danube proclaim Septimius Severus emperor; Severus marches on Rome; Julianus killed **197** Severus absolute ruler after victory over rivals		
200		**c. 200** Christian writer Clemens from Alexandria; triumphal arch of Septimius Severus in Rome	
205			
210	**211** Death of Septimius Severus in Britain, succeeded by both his sons, Caracalla and Geta **211-217** Caracalla **212** Geta murdered, Caracalla absolute ruler	**c. 210** Legal scholars Papinian and Ulpian in Rome; works by Philostratus; construction of the Baths of Caracalla in Rome; Roman history by the Greek Cassius Dio	
215	**217** Caracalla killed by soldier in Syria; Praetorian Prefect Macrinus succeeds him **218** Mutiny of Roman army in Syria: Macrinus defeated and killed; Elagabalus proclaimed emperor **218-222** Elagabalus emperor in Rome **222-235** Alexander Severus		
220			**220** Fall of the Han dynasty in China; invasions by northern nomads; start of partition of China into subkingdoms, migration of Turkish nomads through the steppes of Asia from east to west; temporary end of the Silk Route
225		**c. 225** Christian catacomb paintings in Rome; works by the Christian scholar Origen	**226** Fall of the Parthians; succeeded by the Sassanid dynasty; the New Persian Empire; wars with the Roman Empire
230			
235	**235-285** Period of anarchy; the soldier-emperors		
240			

Prehistoric Times	Antiquity	Middle Ages	Renaissance	Modern History	Contemporary History

ROME POLITICAL HISTORY	ROME CULTURAL HISTORY	EVENTS IN THE REST OF THE WORLD
249-251 Decius as emperor; general order to worship Roman gods results in Christian persecution; Decius killed by the Goths **253-260** Valerian **257** Start of new Christian persecution **260** Valerian taken prisoner by the Persians **263-268** Gallienus; Palmyra and Gaul declare themselves independent **270-275** Aurelian; restoration of empire unity **276-284** Soldier-emperors Probus, Carus, Carinus, Numerian continue Aurelian policies **284** Diocles proclaimed emperor; changes name to Diocletian. Start of large-scale reorganization and consolidation in the Empire **285** Maximian made co-emperor in the west: start of multiple emperorships	**c. 260** Works by Plotinus, founder of the Neo-Platonic school **274** Temple of the Sun in Rome consecrated by Aurelian **c. 300** Diocletian's Thermae in Rome; palace of Diocletian in Spalato (Split, Croatia) with monument to the Tetrarchs; works by the Christian historian Eusebius of Caesarea	 **c. 250** Expansion of the Jews, Christians and Manichaeans from west to central to eastern Asia; increasing Buddhist influence in China **c. 300** Start of the Gupta dynasty in India; Sanskrit literature and Indian visual art flourish; start of Indian influence on southeast Asia

240 — 245 — 250 — 255 — 260 — 265 — 270 — 275 — 280 — 285 — 290 — 295 — 300 — 305 — 310

| Prehistoric Times | Antiquity | Middle Ages | Renaissance | Modern History | Contemporary History |

Glossary

Actium place on the Greek northwest coast near where Octavian defeated the fleet of Antony and Cleopatra in 31 BC. This victory gave Octavian definitive power as Roman emperor.

adopted emperors emperors of the second century AD, adopted by their predecessors; chosen as successors because of their own organizational and military capacities. Trajan was the first.

aedile civil servant at executive level in the republic of Rome; in charge of public order, the market, water and grain provisions, and public games; one-year term.

Aeneas legendary forefather of the Julian line and of the Roman people; fled with his son Julus out of the destroyed city of Troy; established a new empire in Latium; the main character in Virgil's epic *Aeneid.*

Africa the territory on the northern shore of Africa once belonging to and surrounding the city of Carthage; made a province by Rome after the conquest of Carthage in 146 BC.

Alaric (AD 370-410) king of the Western Goths who conquered Rome after plundering Macedonia and Greece around AD 410.

Alamanni southern German people who repeatedly threatened Gallic borders; invaded Gaul in the third century AD; conquered eastern Gaul at the end of the fourth century AD.

Antony, Mark (Marcus Antonius) (82-30 BC) a member of the Second Triumvirate; defeated Caesar's murderers in 42 BC, afterward holding power in the East. Through the intrigues of the ambitious Egyptian Queen Cleopatra, he fell into conflict with Octavian, who defeated him at Actium in 31 BC.

aqueduct literally, conductor of water; Roman system to transport water long distances in mains supported by high arched constructions. The water drained into large basins which led to public fountains.

Ara pacis Augustae altar on the Campus Martius built by Augustus after his return from Spain and Gaul. Consecrated in 9 BC, it was intended to serve as propaganda for Augustus's policy of peace.

Arabia Felix (Happy Arabia) empire in the south of present-day Arabia. It traded gold, spices and incense and formed a link in the caravan trade with India and the Far East.

arena literally meaning "the sand"; the part of the amphitheater where the audience sat around in tiered rows.

Augustus honorary title granted to Octavian by the Senate in 27 BC when he set aside the extraordinary qualifications inherent in his name. *Augustus* ("exalted") is a religious epithet for superhuman. His successors adopted Augustus as a fixed title.

bacaudae armies of escaped coloni (tenant famers).

Batavians a German group from the region between the Rhine and the Meuse. They helped the Romans to subjugate the area and served in the Roman army. In AD 69 they revolted under Julius Civilis, but were quickly defeated.

Britain area inhabited by the Celts, occupied and conquered after AD 43 under Claudius following attempts by Caesar in 55-54 BC. In 125, Hadrian's Wall was built as a northern border. The Romans left Britain around the year AD 400.

Brutus, Marcus Junius (85-42 BC) Brutus supported Pompey in the civil war, was pardoned and became Caesar's favorite. In 44 BC, he led the plot against Caesar and killed him, together with Cassius. He committed suicide after being defeated by Antony in 42.

Byzantium city on the Bosporus which became the residence of Constantine; became known as Constantinople (present-day Istanbul) in AD 330. Byzantium was an important political and cultural center. In 395, it was made capital of the eastern Roman Empire and, later, of the Byzantine Empire.

caesar title used by emperors after Augustus Caesar.

Caesar, Gaius Julius (100-44 BC) After setting up the First Triumvirate in 60 BC, he became governor of Gaul in 58; expanded Transalpine Gaul as far as the Rhine. Caesar conquered Italy with his army and started a civil war. In 46, holding power over the entire empire, he became dictator. He was murdered by a Republican conspiracy in 44.

Caligula, Gaius Caesar (AD 12-41) Roman emperor 37-41, son of Gemanicus, Caligula (literally, little soldier's boot, a nickname from his youth) behaved like a Hellenistic sovereign, demanding divine adoration. After a four-year reign of terror, he was murdered by his bodyguard.

Campius Martius a field on the banks of the Tiber River, dedicated to Mars, where military exercises, sports, games and public meetings were held. Many temples and other public buildings were erected there during the Principate.

canticum a sung text.

Caracalla, Marcus Aurelius Antoninus (AD 188-217) Roman emperor 211-217.

Carthage capital of the Carthaginian Empire in North Africa; conquered by Rome and made the central city of the Roman province named Africa in 146 BC.

castra a specially fortified army camp, often permanent, surrounded by a moat and an earthen rampart; noted for its geometric organization plan. Permanent camps on the borders were built of stone.

Catiline (Lucius Sergius Catilina) (108-62 BC) Roman politician and conspirator; executed in 62 BC.

Celts a group from Gaul and Britain. Around 400 BC, they entered Spain and northern Italy, destroying Rome. Eventually subjugated by Caesar, those living in Gaul were Romanized.

censor one of two Roman magistrates appointed to take the census, a public inventory of the population for wealth, class division, taxes, and military service. They also passed judgement on moral behavior.

Cerberus mythological three-headed dog that guarded the passage to the underworld.

Cicero, Marcus Tullius (106-43 BC) famous Roman lawyer, orator, and author of philosophical and political works; challenged Catiline as consul in 60 BC, supported Pompey in the civil war in 49 BC, and took sides against Antony in 44. He was murdered in 43 BC on Antony's order.

Circus Maximus a large racecourse in Rome at the foot of the Palatine Hill, where chariot races were held as a source of amusement to the public. The circus was also used as a political safety valve; the public would applaud or jeer the charioteer favored by the emperor to indicate their support for the emperor himself.

civitas sine suffragio citizenship without the right to vote.

civitates self-governing autonomous communities.

Claudius, Tiberius Claudius Drusus Nero Germanicus (AD 10-54) Roman emperor 41-54; started the conquest of Britain and the construction of the port at Ostia. His wife Agrippina murdered him to benefit her son Nero.

Cleopatra (69-30 BC) Queen of Egypt 51-49; mistress of Julius Caesar and Mark Antony; defeated by Octavian at the battle of Actium in 31, she later took her own life.

collegia early forms of trade guilds.

colonus the small tenant farmer of a great Roman estate. Always dependent on the large landowners, in AD 332, the coloni were forced by law to stay on the land as serfs.

colonia civilian settlement established to Romanize or control subjugated areas. The colonists were mainly ex-military and remained Roman citizens. Examples of such settlements are Carthage, Corinth, and Cologne.

853

Colosseum the great Roman amphitheater where the gladiators fought and the circus games took place. Named after the large statue of Nero, the Colossus.

Constantinople a name for Byzantium (present-day Istanbul) which became the (Christian) residence of the Emperor Constantine in AD 330. In 395 it was made the capital of the eastern Roman Empire.

Constantine I, Flavius Valerius (AD 280-337) called the Great, first Christian Roman emperor 306-337.

consul either of two chief magistrates of the Roman Republic appointed annually.

Corinth A Greek town destroyed in 146 BC for its resistance to Roman suppression. Rebuilt in 44 BC on Caesar's order as capital of the Roman colony Achaea.

Dacia an area north of the Danube (present-day Rumania) subjugated by Trajan and made into a province after several wars in AD 106.

damnatio memoriae damned in memory; the removal from the official records of one's reign.

Decius (AD 201-251) emperor from AD 249 to 251. Systematic persecution of Christians took place for the first time under his reign. They refused to obey his edict making it compulsory for all Romans to worship the state deities.

dictator a magistrate appointed by the consuls, given unlimited power in emergencies in state affairs and military matters, originally for a six-month term. As dictators during the civil wars, Sulla and Caesar held an unassailable position of power for an unlimited duration.

Diocletian (Gaius Aurelius Valerius Diocletianus) (AD 245-313) Roman emperor AD 284-305, originator of the concept of tetrarchy.

Domitian (Titus Flavius Domitianus) (AD 51-96) Roman emperor AD 81-96. Noted for his reign of terror.

Druids Celtic priests in Gaul and Britain who held significant power due to their religious and medical knowledge and sorcery. They led the resistance against the Roman conquerors.

duumviri a provincial office comparable to the consulate in Rome. Shared by two members of the local aristocracy, they were in charge of a town for the period of one year.

Eastern Roman Empire From the 6th to the 15th century AD, called the Byzantine Empire, it was the eastern segment of the Roman Empire, divided after the death of Emperor Theodosius (AD 395).

edict an official order given by the emperor. Famous examples are Diocletian's price-control edict and Constantine's edict of Milan, which granted freedom of religion.

epic a narrative poem about mythological heroes, written in hexameter verse. Best-known examples are Homer's *Iliad* and *Odyssey* (Greek) and Virgil's *Aeneid* (Latin).

equites the name of second-ranking Roman class, originally made up of cavalrymen, it also included traders and bankers.

Etruscans the people from Etruria who ruled much of the Italian peninsula between the 7th and 5th centuries BC.

forum marketplace and public square of an ancient Roman town or city; political, cultural, and commercial center.

Gallia (Gaul) land of the Gauls; Cisalpine Gaul (northern Italy) was conquered in 200 BC. Gallia Narbonensis (Provence) was colonized in 118 BC. Transalpine Gaul (France, Belgium) was conquered by Caesar (58-53 BC).

Germans European peoples from the north of the Rhine. Caesar drove out the Germans below the Rhine.

gladiator a man (often a slave or convicted criminal) in ancient Rome who fought to the death for public amusement in amphitheaters; opponents could be other gladiators or wild animals.

Goths a German group in the third century AD. Living in Dacia, they were feared plunderers threatening the Roman borders. In the 4th century AD, the West Goths were driven back by the Huns. The Romans granted them permission to settle below the Danube. About 400, they attacked Rome under the leadership of Alaric. The East Goths were conquered by the Huns and later moved to Hungary.

Gregorian calendar Pope Gregory XIII changed the Julian calendar in 1582, considering the years too long. He ordered leap year dropped at the turn of the century (with the exception of the millennium). In order to catch up, the days between the 4th and 15th of October, 1582, were canceled.

Hadrian (Publius Aelius Hadrianus) (AD 76-138) adopted by Trajan. He consolidated the borders of the empire and suppressed a Jewish rebellion.

Hadrian's Wall masonry wall built by Hadrian (AD 120-123) to protect Roman Britain from northern peoples; runs from Solway Firth to the Tyne.

hexameter A form of verse used mainly in epic poems, consisting of six dactylic and spondaic feet. (A dactyl consists of one long and two short syllables; a spondee has two long syllables.)

homo novus the first in a Roman family to hold the offices of quaestor, aedile, praetor, and finally consul.

Horace (Quintus Horatius Flaccus) (65-8 BC) Latin poet; his work, inspired by Greek poetry, includes odes, satires, the didactic poem on poetry *Ars Poetica*, and the chorus of *Carmen Saeculare*.

imperator original title of a general after the victory that gave him the right to a triumphal procession. Augustus and his successors adopted this title as a first name, so that imperator became the title of the highest commander.

imperium originally, military authority given to Roman generals and consuls; later included the right to call together and speak before the Senate and the people's assembly; also denotes the sphere of power.

infamia a bad public reputation.

insula lower-class housing; badly constructed apartment buildings packed into poor districts of Rome. Densely populated, they were often hit by large fires.

Isis Egyptian goddess of fertility and, by extension, of the heavens and nature. The Romans became acquainted with the worship of Isis around 100 BC. During the Principate she had many followers, among them the Emperor Caligula.

Julian calendar Introduced in 46 BC by Julius Caesar, this had a year comprised of 365 days with one extra day every fourth year. Before this, a year consisted of 355 days with a 22 or 23-day leap month every other year.

Julian (Flavius Claudius Julianus) (AD 331-363) called *Apostata* (the Unfaithful), Roman emperor 355-363, he favored the Roman gods and limited the rights of the Christians and the influence of the Church.

Jupiter god of the sky, thunder, and lightening; the highest of Roman deities, he controlled the universe; identified with the Greek god Zeus.

Lares spirits of departed ancestors; guardian deities of private homes and estates. Each house had a chapel or altar for sacrifices to the Lares, who also protected roads and travelers. A *lararium* was a room containing statues of the house spirits.

latifundia large, economically independent estates originally worked by slaves. When plantation size increased, they were developed using coloni who leased some land in exchange for part of the harvest.

Latin originally, the language of Latium and Rome. As Rome's power grew, Latin became the official language of the western Roman Empire. Greek continued to be spoken in the eastern part.

legion Roman army division made up of 6,000 infantrymen and 300 cavalry, originally all Roman citizens. During the Principate there were approximately 25 legions. Non-

Romans served with the *auxilia* (backup troops). Some soldiers received citizenship after serving in a legion.

Livy (Titus Livius) (59 BC-AD 17) Latin historian who wrote an extensive work, partially preserved, on the history of Rome from its foundation in 753 BC (*Ab Urbe Condita*).

ludi magni Large games in honor of Jupiter, held annually from 366 BC. The festivities, originally religious in nature, included theatrical performances, circus games, and competitions.

Maecenas, Gaius Cilnius (70-8 BC) Roman statesman, friend, and employee of Augustus, especially known for supporting talented artists and writers, like Virgil and Horatius.

Marcus Aurelius Antoninus (AD 121-180) Roman emperor 161-180, adopted by Antoninus Pius.

mare nostrum political and propaganda term for the Mediterranean ("our sea") and the surrounding area used by the Romans for their sphere of power.

Marius, Gaius (156-86 BC) Roman successful general and consul; lead the opposition against the Senate and Sulla. In 87 BC, his party of the plebs took over power and imposed a reign of terror in Rome.

Mars god of war and the forces; father of the mythical founders of Rome, Romulus and Remus; protector of Rome; identified with the Greek god Ares.

mausoleum a monumental tomb. Augustus had a large mausoleum built in 28 BC for the imperial family at the Campus Martius. Hadrian had his built on the opposite bank of the Tiber in AD 130.

Mercury god of trade, merchants, and travelers; identified with the Greek god Hermes.

Mesopotamia the area between the Euphrates and Tigris Rivers; inhabited by the Parthians in Roman times.

Metamorphoses poetical work (stories from Greek mythology) by Ovid.

municipia Originally non-Roman, these were subjugated cities managed in Roman fashion and integrated into the empire.

myth a story handed down from oral tradition about deities and supernatural beings, closely connected to the culture of a people.

Nero Claudius Drusus Germanicus Caesar (AD 37-68) emperor from 54 to 68. In 59 he had his mother Agrippina murdered and forced his supposed opponents to suicide. Noted for extravagant behavior, Nero encountered great resistance from the upper ranks. When a large part of Rome was destroyed by fire in 64, he blamed the Christians and prosecuted them for arson. In

68, the army revolted; Nero committed suicide.

nobiles a class in the Republic, comprised of patricians and rich plebeians, which controlled administrative power. Consuls and other magistrates were chosen from among them.

numen divine power, will, or function, not connected to a specific god. In Roman religion, divine expression of will was more important than divine personality.

Octavian (Gaius Julius Caesar Octavianus) (63 BC-AD 14) adopted son of Caesar, he defeated Caesar's murderers with the help of a triumvirate, taking power in the west. He defeated Antony at the battle of Actium in 31 BC. Granted extraordinary powers by the Senate to restore the Republic, he set them aside in 27 BC, but remained in power as princeps and, in fact, as the first Roman emperor. He restructured the empire, restored old norms and values, modernized Rome, and fostered a policy of peace.

Optimates the conservative Senate party in the second and first centuries BC; opponents of the people's party (Populares), which favored reform.

Ostia port on the mouth of the Tiber River. Expanded under Emperor Claudius, Ostia became a international port and a transit harbor for the grain supplies to Rome.

Ovid (Publius Ovidius Naso) (43 BC-AD 18) Roman poet who wrote *Metamorphoses;* banished by Emperor Augustus in part because of his work.

Palatine oldest inhabited hill in Rome, home of the imperial palaces of Augustus, Tiberius, Domitian, and Septimius Severus. At the foot of the Palatine was the Forum Romanum.

panem et circenses (bread and circuses) term first used by Juvenal referring to the upperclass conviction that this was all the common people needed to remain content. Grain was distributed to the proletariat and the games were funded by the state.

Pantheon a round temple dedicated to all the gods of the empire. Originally built by Agrippa on the Campus Martius, it was destroyed several times and later rebuilt by Domitian, Hadrian, and Septimius Severus. Later, it was used as a Christian church.

Parthians Iranian horsemen who lived in Asia from the second century BC on. They defeated Crassus and Antony, carried on wars regularly during the Principate, and were finally conquered by the Persians in the third century AD.

patricians a small group of families who held all management and religious functions at the beginning of the Republic. Gradually, they had to give way to the lower plebeians, indispensable to the defense of Rome. From

287 BC, plebeian decisions were regarded as equal to patrician laws.

pax Augusta the peace Augustus glorified in propaganda, illustrated by his altar to it, the *ara pacis.* In reality, he carried out conquests in Europe to the banks of the Danube.

Persians Iranian mounted people who controlled a large empire in Asia until conquered by Alexander the Great around 330 BC. A great Persian Empire arose again in the 3rd century AD, replacing the Parthians and waging incessant war with the Romans.

plebeians the masses in Rome who had no influence initially, but because of their military importance, were made equal in political status to the patricians in 287 BC. Rich plebeians shared power with the patricians from the 4th century BC onward.

Pompeii a southern Italian city which was covered by ash and lava when Mt. Vesuvius erupted in AD 79. Never rebuilt, the city was excavated beginning in 1860. It offers a picture of Roman daily life.

Pompey (Gaius Pompeius Magnus) (106-48 BC): Roman general and statesman; set up the First Triumvirate with Caesar and Crassus in 60 BC.

pontifex maximus head of the college of priests responsible for the state religion. During the Principate, the emperor was also *pontifex maximus.*

Pontius Pilate (Pilatus) procurator of the province of Judaea AD 26-36 when Jesus was crucified.

praetor Roman civil servant during Republic, directly under the consul.

Praetorian Guard imperial bodyguard.

princeps "first citizen," originally the name for senators holding most power; adopted as an imperial title.

proconsul Roman official with consular authority who commanded an army and frequently served as governor of a senatorial province.

proletariat lowest class in ancient Roman society; people who did not own property.

propraetor former Roman praetor sent to govern a province.

province conquered area outside Italy developed for the benefit of Rome.

Punic Wars waged between Rome and Carthage for power in the Mediterranean region from 264-241, 218-201, and 149-146 BC; they ended with the destruction of Carthage.

quaestor originally, a Roman official who judged certain criminal cases; later, a civil servant in charge of finances. The quaestorship was the beginning of a political career.

res publica "public thing"; name of the Roman state between 509 and 31 BC.

Rhine River in Germany and the Netherlands, this formed the northern border of the Roman Empire from the time of Augustus on.

Saturn god of agriculture; also worshipped by the Romans as the bringer of culture and affluence; identified with the Greek god Cronus.

Scythians nomadic people of Iranian descent who settled in southern Russia in the 8th century BC; noted equestrians and archers.

Senate the supreme council of ancient Rome; originally comprised of patricians only, it came to include the lower plebeians.

Seneca, Lucius Annaeus (4 BC-AD 65) Latin writer and Stoic philosopher, Seneca was a teacher and advisor to Nero between 49 and 62. He retired in 62 and was ordered to commit suicide by Nero in 65. Noted for his tragedies; his philosophical works include *De Ira, De Clementia,* and *Epistulae Morales.*

sesterces monetary unit used by the Romans.

soldier-emperors Roman emperors drawn from the military, particularly between AD 235 and 270.

Spartacus (?-71 BC) Thracian gladiator who led a slave rebellion against Rome in 73 BC.

Stoicism Greek school of philosophy founded by Zeno in 308 BC; holds that all happenings are the free result of divine will and that man should, therefore, calmly accept his fate, free of passion, joy, or grief. Self-control and austerity are emphasized. Stoicism was fashionable in the first century BC and during the first centuries of the Principate.

Sulla, Lucius Cornelius (138-78 BC) Roman general and dictator.

tetrarchy The rule of four emperors put into effect by Diocletian in AD 293; divided imperial power between two primary leaders called Augustus, assisted by two Caesars who were also their successors.

thermae public gathering places with cold, lukewarm and hot baths, sport schools, training fields and sometimes libraries. Most famous are the Baths of Caracalla, built between AD 212 and 216 in Rome.

Tiber River flows southward through central Italy and Rome to the Mediterranean Sea at Ostia.

Tiberius Claudius Nero (42 BC-AD 37) Roman emperor AD 14-37.

Trajan (Marcus Ulpius Trajanus) (AD 52-117) Roman emperor 98-117.

tribunus plebis (tribune of the plebeians) any of several Roman magistrates appointed after 494 BC to protect the rights of the plebeians from the power of the patricians. After these two groups were given equal status (287 BC), the tribunus plebis became the representative of all the people and was closely involved with political decision-making. Caesar and Augustus derived their constitutional authority mainly from function as tribunus plebis.

triumvirate a Roman three-man state commission with a special task. In 60 BC, Pompey, Crassus, and Caesar formed the first; in 43 BC, Octavian, Lepidus, and Antony formed the Second Triumvirate.

urbs Latin word for city, but also a reference to Rome as the capital of the Roman Empire.

usurper one who unlawfully assumes the throne.

Venus goddess of fertility, love, and spring; identified with the Greek goddess Aphrodite. During the Principate, Venus was honored as ancestress of the Julian line of emperors because she was the mother of Aeneas, the forefather of Rome.

Vespasian (Titus Flavius Sabinus Vespasianus) (AD 9-79) Roman emperor 69-79: under his rule, both the Jewish uprising and the Batavian rebellion were crushed.

Vestal virgins six female priests of the goddess Vesta, goddess of hearthfire and symbol of the Roman state; these were required to take vows of chastity and look after the sacred fire in the Temple of Vesta.

Via Appia oldest and most important Roman road, constructed by Appius Claudius Caecus in 312 BC, it ran from Rome to Capua and insured success in the battle against the Samnites.

Virgil (Publius Vergilius Maro) (70-19 BC) Latin poet, author of *The eclogues* (The Pastoral) and *Georgica,* his didactic poem on agriculture, and the epic *Aeneid.* It tells the story of the legendary Aeneas, illustrating predestination in Rome's growth to a world power.

Western Roman Empire western part of the Roman Empire, divided in AD 395.

Bibliography

The End of the Republic
F.E. Adcock, *Marcus Crassus, Millionaire*, Cambridge 1966.
M. Gelzer, *Caesar, Politician and Statesman*, Oxford 1968.
P. Greenhalgh, *Pompey*, 2 vols. London 1980-81.
A. Keaveney, *Lucullus, a Life*, London 1992.
A.W. Lintott, *Violence in Republican Rome*, Oxford 1968.
D.C.A. Shotter, *The Fall of the Roman Republic*, London 1994.
D.L. Stockton, *Cicero: a Political Biography*, Oxford 1971.

From Caesar to Augustus
E. Bradford, *Julius Caesar: The Pursuit of Power*, London 1984.
M.L. Clarke, *The Noblest Roman: Marcus Brutus and His Reputation*, London 1981.
E. Gruen, *The Last Generation of the Roman Republic*, Berkeley 1974.
E. Huzar, *Mark Antony, a Biography*, Minnesota 1978.
D.C.A. *Shotter, Augustus Caesar*, London 1991.
R. Syme, *The Roman Revolution*, Oxford 1939.
L.R. Taylor, *Party Politics in the Age of Caesar*, Berkeley 1944.

Dictatorship
G.W. Bowersock, *Augustus and the Greek World*, Oxford 1965.
D. Earl, *The Age of Augustus*, London 1968.
D. Kienast, *Augustus, Prinzeps und Monarch*, Darmstadt 1982.
G. Rickman, *The Corn Supply of Ancient Rome*, Oxford 1980.
D.C.A. Shotter, *Augustus Caesar*, London 1991.
R. Syme, *The Roman Revolution*, Oxford 1939.
C.M. Wells, *The German Policy of Augustus*, Oxford 1972.

The First Emperors
J.P.V.D. Balsdon, *The Emperor Gaius*, Oxford 1934.
A. Barrett, *Caligula: the Corruption of Power*, London 1989.
B. Levick, *Tiberius the Politician*, London 1976.
B. Levick, *Claudius*, London 1989.
A. Momigliano, *Claudius: the Emperor and His Achievement*, Oxford 1961.
R. Seager, *Tiberius*, London 1972.
Z. Yavetz, *Plebs and Princeps*, Oxford 1969.

Consolidation of Power
P.A.L. Greenhalgh, *The Year of the Four Emperors, Galba, Otho, Vitellius and Vespasian*, London 1975.
M. Griffin, *Nero: the End of a Dynasty*, London 1984.
L. Homo, *Vespasien, l'empereur du bon sens*, Paris 1949.
B.W. Jones, *The Emperor Titus*, London 1984.

E.M. Smallwood, *The Jews under Roman Rule*, Leiden 1976.
K. Wellesley, *The Long Year AD 69*, London 1975.

Romanization of the Empire
A. Birley, *Marcus Aurelius*, London 1966.
B.W. Jones, *The Emperor Domitian*, London 1992.
F.A. Lepper, *Trajan's Parthian War*, Oxford 1948.
F. Millar, *The Emperor in the Roman World*, London 1977.
B. d'Orgeval, *L'Empereur Hadrien*, Paris 1950.
H.M.D. Parker, *A History of the Roman World from AD 138 to AD 337*, London 1958.
S. Perowne, *Hadrian*, London 1986.

Life in Rome
K.R. Bradley, *Slaves and Masters in the Roman Empire*, Brussels 1984.
R.P. Duncan-Jones, *The Economy of the Roman Empire*, Cambridge 1974.
B.W. Frier, *Landlords and Tenants in Imperial Rome*, Princeton 1980.
J. Liversidge, *Everyday Life in the Roman Empire*, London 1978.
R. MacMullen, *Roman Social Relations, 50 BC - AD 284*, New Haven 1974.
G. Rickman, *The Corn Supply of Ancient Rome*, Oxford 1980.
Z. Yavets, *Slaves and Slavery in Ancient Rome*, Oxford 1987.

Bread and Games
J.P.V.D. Balsdon, *Life and Leisure in Ancient Rome*, Bodley Head 1969.
A. Cameron, *Circus Factions: Blues and Greens at Rome and Byzantium*, Oxford 1966.
J. Carcopino, *Daily Life in Ancient Rome*, Harmondsworth 1956.
L. Friedländer, *Roman Life and Manners under the Early Empire*, Leipzig 1920.
M. Grant, *Gladiators*, Harmondsworth 1967.
J. Humphrey, *Roman Circuses and Chariot Racing*, London 1986.
P. Veyne, *Le pain et le cirque*, Paris 1976.

Decline in Power
G.C. Brauer Jr., *The Age of the Soldier Emperors*, Park Ridge N.J. 1975.
A.R. Birley, *The African Emperor Septimius Severus*, London 1988.
W.H.C. Frend, *Martyrdom and Persecution in the Early Church*, New York 1966.
M. Grant, *The Climax of Rome: the Final Achievement of the Ancient World, AD 161 - 337*, Boston 1968.

R. MacMullen, *Roman Government's Response to Crisis,* New Haven 1976.
J. Vogt, *The Decline of Rome,* New York 1967.

The Late Empire
T.D. Barnes, *Constantine and Eusebius,* Cambridge Mass. 1981.
D. van Berchem, *L'armée de Dioclétien et la réforme constantinienne,* Paris 1952.
R.L. Fox, *Pagans and Christians,* London 1986.
A.H.M. Jones, *The Later Roman Empire,* 3 vol. Oxford 1964.
A.H.M. Jones, *The Decline of the Ancient World,* London 1966.
W. Seston, *Dioclétien et la tétrarchie,* Paris 1946.

S. Williams, *Diocletian and the Roman Recovery,* London 1985.

Allies and Enemies
J.P.V.D. Balsdon, *Romans and Aliens,* London 1979.
L. Casson, *The Periplus Maris Erythraei,* Princeton 1989.
J.I. Miller, *The Spice Trade of the Roman Empire, 29 BC - AD 641,* Oxford 1969.
J.S. Romm, *The Edges of the Earth in Ancient Thought: Geography, Exploration and Fiction,* Princeton 1992.
J.W. Sedlar, *India and the Greek World,* Totowa N.J. 1980.
N.H.H. Sitwell, *Outside the Empire: the World the Romans Knew,* London 1984.
M. Todd, *The Northern Barbarians, 100 BC - AD 300,* London 1975.

Illustration Credits

Index